The World is
WATCHING

TREEHOUSE
b o o k s

1430 W. Susquehanna Ave
Philadelphia, PA 19121
215-236-1760 | treehousebooks.org

The World is
WATCHING

EDITED BY
David Robinson, Alice Palmer and
Edward L. "Buzz" Palmer

FOREWORD BY
Haki R. Madhubuti

Third World Press Foundation
Chicago, Illinois

Third World Press Foundation
Publishers since 1967
Chicago
© Copyright 2019 Edward "Buzz" Palmer and Alice J. Palmer

Printed in the United States of America
ISBN: 978-0-88378- 408-2
Library of Congress number on file
22 21 20 19 18   6 5 4 3 2 1

Conceived by:
Edward L. "Buzz" Palmer
Edited by:
David B. Robinson and Alice J. Palmer
Project Editor:
Melissa Moore, Associate Editor of Special Projects
Designer:
Denise Borel Billups
Cover art compilation art by istockphoto.com

Ohio U Professor Emeritus Robert Rhodes; Alice Palmer; Black United Fund of
IL CEO Henry English; Dr. Doudou Diene, Special Rapporteur on Race, UN.;
Edward "Buzz" Palmer

| v |

ACKNOWLEDGEMENTS

To those who have passed on who were integral to our lives and work:

Richard Durham; Jan Carew; Ishmael Flores; Louis Martin; Harold Washington; Vernon Jarrett; Sen. Paul Simon, Dr. Robb Meir, Dr. Robert Cummings; Elworth Taylor; Pastor Tyrone Cryder; Gus Savage; Henry English; Robert Rhodes; John Casey; Ibrahim Abu Lughod; Judith Martin-Wambu; Prime Minister Olaf Palme, Prime Minister Michael Manley; Frederick Douglass Andrews; Pauline Morton-Finney; Lerone Bennett Jr. and his son Lerone Bennett III; Otto Palmer; Erskine Roberts; Mary Ward Roberts; Ben and Lillian Robinson; Eqbal Ahmad; Rafael Moseev; Talmadge Betts; John Stroger; Chauncey Bailey; Eugene Sawyer; Georgia and Lou Palmer; Lou Jones; Dorothy Jefferson; Ald. Michael Scott; Ben Butler; Manfred Stassen; Dr. Joseph H. Ward; Paul Booth; Kearnie Anderson; Maggie Jackson; Richard Newhouse; Katherine Mays; Mrs. Zella Louise Locklear Ward; Sandra Carpenter; and Cedric Herring.

We also wish to acknowledge the incredible team at Third World Press Foundation for their insights, commitment, and assistance in putting this book together. Georgia Rae Lasio also deserves our profound thanks for taking knotted tangles of pictures and prose and putting them into a form that we could use.

And to the many who continue to inform our lives and work who are too numerous to name.

Edward "Buzz" Palmer, Alice J. Palmer, and David B. Robinson

CONTENTS

Acknowledgements   vi

An Ode to the late John Casey   ix

To the Late Dr. Manfred Stassen   x

Foreword   xi
    Haki R. Madhubuti

Preface: Why This Book, Why Now   xiii
    Edward "Buzz" Palmer and Alice J. Palmer

"The Furious Reverberations of Freedom: xv
Global Impressions of African-Americans Today"
    David B. Robinson

SECTION ONE-FROM THERE

GERMANY
    Manfred Stassen   3
    Berndt Ostendorf   8

UNITED KINGDOM
    Glynn Ford   15
    Lord Meghnad Desai   19
    Florence Kabba   23

DENMARK
    Peter Plenge   27

FINLAND
    Kaarle Nordenstreng   34

THE NETHERLANDS
    John P. Kraal   37

AFRICA

Nigeria – Dr. Shaffdeen Amuwo   41

Kenya – Christopher K. Wambu   61

Senegal – Doudou Diène   74

INDIA

Shashi Tharoor   88

Ramu Damodaran   94

SINGAPORE

Shantoba Eliza Carew-Edwin   105

SECTION TWO - FROM HERE

WASHINGTON, D.C.

Richard Rubenstein   113

LOUISVILLE, KENTUCKY

Joy Gleason Carew, PhD   119

CHICAGO

Loren Taylor   123

Chef Sara Louise Phillips   143

Marvinetta Penn   160

Teresa Córdova   164

AN ODE TO THE LATE JOHN CASEY

l-r JOHN Casey, Secretary General of the World Alliance of YMCA's; Pope John Paul II
PHOTO COURTESY OF JOHN CASEY

John was with me in trenches to give voice and power to those without either. John practiced real statecraft, power without bombast or glee after victory, only moving on to the next task. John consulted and advised many world leaders, including a pope; and even as a good Irishman was invited to events with the Queen of England.

Always appearing unassuming, hiding what he was: a man of steel. I will never forget him telling me about his confronting a former U.S. attorney general, who mistakenly believed that he could bulldoze John and didn't see the steel hidden in his unassuming persona. The man learned what steel is, to his regret. John headed one of the largest non-governmental organizations in the world, the World Alliance of YMCAs, in Geneva, Switzerland. While he spoke quietly, world leaders listened. There was never any gloating over a well-earned victory. John was masterful and my friend.

l-r Homer Franklin, President of Olive-Harvey College, Chicago; Buzz Palmer, JOHN Casey
PHOTO BY DAVID ROBINSON

Rest in Peace. You earned it.

Your eternal friend,

Buzz

TO THE LATE
DR. MANFRED STASSEN

My mentor, counselor and great friend Manfred Stassen was a giant. I first met him when he was the Director of the German Academic Exchange Service (DAAD) in the United States.

Manfred told me that his life and his family's lives were saved by Black American GIs who—during the Winter Hunger after WWII in Germany, when millions died of starvation—fed him and his family.

Searching for food in Germany during this time, young Manfred would take leavings from garbage cans behind American GI mess halls. The white soldiers who saw him digging in the garbage cans would defecate and urinate on the garbage. Black soldiers, seeing him, asked Manfred if he and his family were hungry, then they gave him food. Manfred said these soldiers kept his family alive.

Later, Manfred had a choice to be an academic or, as he put it, march through the corridors of power.

Manfred was a major member of the trio that represented Germany internationally during the Brandt era, along with the chancellor of Germany and the chairman of Mercedes-Benz. While teaching at Johns Hopkins University in Maryland during the 1980s, the Chinese ambassador to the United States asked him to advise Chinese leadership on how to develop a market economy and how to integrate Hong Kong into Mainland China. He was also a frequent lecturer in India, and he had been asked to develop a new university in Kashmir, India.

Over the years, Manfred arranged for me to meet German leaders in business, academia and non government organizations. Manfred vetted all my international initiatives. He gave my initiatives the same attention that he gave those of the German chancellor, India's president, and the Chinese politburo. When I came up with an initiative that he particularly liked, he paid me the compliment of saying, "I should have thought of that."

I will forever miss him.

FOREWORD
CLEAN VISION, OPEN PATHS

Haki R. Madhubuti

With the illegal election of the 45th president of the United States, most literate and political Americans find themselves in a national and international quandary. In their contemplation, on the current state of their nation and the world, there is deep worry. Also, with 45's decision to pull out of the Paris Climate Agreement as fires, floods, and human migrations reorder the landscapes of too many nations, it is expected that confusion and fear will occupy their minds, and explode mass media headlines and twitter feeds across the world. That the national budgets of this nation is now in the hands of a corporate welfare and tax giveaway president and deeply compromised congress, demands that the 99% must become even more vigilant, active and creative in planning responses and pro-actions.

One of the un-discussed problems in the national and international Black world is our ignorance of foreign affairs. This ignorance has been an accepted reality, I have given some attention to this critical deficiency in my own work[1]. A recent example of this knowledge "white out" is the recent passing of the former Secretary-General of the United Nations, the honorable Kofi Annan, the first African to lead that international body. His tenure at the United Nations encouraged many of the world's people to put diplomacy in their day to day conversations. As we acknowledge his contributions, I am happy to strongly recommend a new book, *The World is Watching* edited by David Robinson, Alice Palmer and Edward L. "Buzz" Palmer. This "autobiographical document" of international struggle, world travel and conversations, remarkable and unfiltered interactions across languages, cultures and continents is both riveting and imperative. If nothing else, both Annan and President Obama encouraged millions of Black diaspora people and others to reconsider our role on the international stage.

We now find our nation in an acute state of stress and confusion. Black, Brown, and all people of color are experiencing hourly attacks from 45 and his supporters and imitators. However, *The World is Watching,* supplies us with clear voices and visions in this climate of white supremacy with its deliberate politics of obfuscation.

This valuable book, with contributors who are both practitioners and theoreticians, arrives with seriousness, containing essays and interviews of men and women with workable answers which have been refined over the years as a result of decades of grassroots, governmental, corporate, university, NGO, and other real-world experiences and confrontations. I use the word confrontations advisedly, Buzz, Alice and their son David have long and unblemished histories of working with all people. I have never known them to shy away from progressive struggles and to always be intimately involved with the burning and drowning issues of our planet.

This book represents a first for us at Third World Press Foundation. As we complete our 51st year, we are honored and fortunate to be able to share with the reading public this magnificent document. The editors, in the tradition of Fredrick Douglass, W.E.B. Du Bois, Monroe Trotter, Alaine Locke, Shirley Graham Du Bois, Ida B. Wells, Malcolm X, John Henrik Clark, Maya Angelou and others, are among the growing many recognizing that people of African ancestry are truly an international people and if we are to be effective in the arena of foreign state craft, *The World is Watching* must be a part of each of our diplomatic portfolios. The deadly arrival of the 21st century requires an awakening of a new, expanded consciousness. We must not only be experienced street fighters but as our best scholars, historians, poets, business people, diplomats, teachers, artists, and political athletes clearly understand—we must engage in trench-like and intellectual warfare simultaneously.

---

[1] *Black Men – Obsolete, Single, Dangerous? The Afrikan American Family in Transition* and. *Taking Bullets – Terrorism and Black Life in Twenty-First Century America Confronting White Nationalism, Supremacy, Privilege, Plutocracy, and Oligarchy* by Haki R. Madhubuti

PREFACE: WHY THIS BOOK, WHY NOW

From Then Til Now: And Still We Rise

Edward "Buzz" Palmer and Alice J. Palmer

Beleaguered and marginalized African Americans have often sought worth outside the United States in the face of debasement by the power elites who have structured African Americans under colonialism, slavery, Jim Crow, and neo-liberalism.

Black Americans created themselves out of the raw pain of slavery, the contradiction of color, the shift from down South to up South northern cities. From the ever present hatred of those who were promised that, no matter their circumstances, they would always be better than niggas. From the eternal fight to be a man, a soldier, a citizen, a worker, Black Americans are an in-spite-of people who took the rhythms of the land and the cities, the organized outcries against injustice, the joyous shouts, the prayers, the resilient, elastic families, and became America's moral compass.

Being Black in America is a journey and a quest for self-affirmation, alliance and place. W. E. B. Dubois called this the twoness of being simultaneously and contradictorily an American and a Black person in America. Black Americans have refused to be acquiescent, and our cry, in the words of Maya Angelou, "And still we rise," has left an indelible imprint at home and abroad.

Out of Black America's fight-back against oppression has risen world recognition and respect. Our arts and sports achievements have enabled our struggle. Our music—jazz and blues—has transfixed the world. Our humanity has not been confined to just our plight, but it reached out to support peoples in far-off countries in their fights for freedom and independence. In token, African American leaders were among the first to support the founding of the United Nations.

However, African Americans—Americans generally—have largely been unaware of how enlightened world figures have viewed and supported Black America's continued struggle for justice and an acknowledgement of their innate humanity.

This book holds up a mirror for Black Americans to see themselves through the eyes of notable men and women outside the United States and Americans who have experiences outside the United States. Their observations and appraisements offer fresh eyes through which Black Americans—especially our young, who are too often victims of parochialism and miasma—can see themselves as world people.

The women and men who have written essays or have been interviewed for this book are special friends and colleagues, whose international perspectives have informed, strengthened and broadened the issues and organizing work we have done over decades.

In this new era, Black Americans are not alone, nor were they in past times. Black Americans have routinely sought allies, solidarity and ideas outside this country. Slaves and free Blacks who saw that it was in their interest to fight against colonialism served in the Royal British Army and in its auxiliary Hessian Army during the American Revolutionary War. When the Hessian soldiers left in 1777, at least one hundred Black men who had served, and their families, left with them to settle in Germany.

Frederick Douglass, while still a slave, made his way to Britain in 1845. For nineteen months, he lectured against U. S. slavery. British abolitionists purchased his freedom, and he was a free man when he returned to America.

Professor Maria Diedrich, a German scholar, has written about the twenty-eight-year liaison between Frederick Douglass and German journalist Ottilie Assing in her book Love Across Color Lines (Hill and Wang, 1999). Their common intellectual interests informed his writings. The relationship ended tragically when Ms. Assing, realizing that Douglass was marrying someone else, committed suicide.

In 1893, Ida B. Wells first went to Britain as a guest of Catherine Impey, a British Quaker, and again in 1894. During the last trip, she finally proved to the British that her accounts of lynching in the United States were true, and she received support for the anti-lynching cause.

The introduction of jazz to Europe and its profound reception when James Reese Europe's band accompanied Black American soldiers to France during World War I have been well documented in numerous books; as has the distinguished service of these Black soldiers—many of whom served in French units when they were shunned by American units. In many respects, the period after World War I in Europe was, in part, informed by the significant presence of Black Americans and their music, art and culture.

Black American writers, artists and performers have continued to travel, work and study abroad, in Europe, Africa and the Caribbean, in their ongoing quest for mutuality.

"THE FURIOUS REVERBERATIONS OF FREEDOM: GLOBAL IMPRESSIONS OF AFRICAN AMERICANS TODAY"

David B. Robinson

Mr. Edward L. "Buzz" Palmer, like so many times before, had arranged for a group of African Americans to visit dignitaries throughout Europe for the exchange of policy and program ideas. The group involved a journalist; a Chicago City Colleges president; a newly-elected U.S. congressman; two educators; the mayor of a small town outside of Chicago; a graduate student, and the CEO of a leading non-profit.

Anyone who joins Buzz on these trips had better eat their Wheaties because the pace and the density of information and activity is like an avalanche. Add the challenge of negotiating several foreign languages, plus non-stop, intense, high-level meetings and you begin to get a picture of how immersive and exhausting these trips can be. For example, we had just taken a train into the exurbs of Amsterdam, but before even arriving that morning, we had already muscled through four days of constant motion.

On day one, we made presentations to the German Embassy in Berlin, met with housing developers in Frankfurt, and visited a university and an incredibly ornate church in Bonn and in Metz, respectively. On the second day, we met with the mayor of London and his staff, who took us on a tour of the city. And later, we visited Parliament, and still later, we took the Tube to enjoy a sumptuous dinner with labor leaders. On day three we met with the head of the socialist party of France and then visited other dignitaries at EU headquarters in Strasburg. While still in France, we met with the President's staff, visited a non-profit in Lyons and sat in on several panel discussions on race and xenophobia. Frustrated young men of color were torching expensive cars throughout the town and we were asked to share our thinking on the causes and the possible solutions. And on day four, we visited a university, wandered through two art museums and one history museum, ate rich foods, drank fine wine in Paris, and caught a jazz show ironically featuring a band from Chicago.

Still reeling from the rush of the past four days, we de-boarded the train and made our way to a housing project on the outskirts of the city of Amsterdam. I couldn't help but notice the similarities in the structure and layout of the buildings to the notorious high-rise monstrosities that once loomed over dirt-poor Black communities in Chicago. These in Amsterdam were at least twenty stories tall and they were clustered together in tight groups of three—nine buildings in all. There was nothing else around them. I noticed an eerie absence of children squealing on playgrounds and there were no major retail stores, no ballfields, no parks, no grass.

Desperate people piled on top of one another in soaring concrete and glass prison cells surrounded by a river, and more concrete and glass carpeting the barren grounds.

"...What you seen...Wasn't no dust of changes rising. It was the dust of sameness settling."

Sterling Plump

A staffer of the mayor of Amsterdam saw us approaching and escorted us into a single-story building that seemed to serve as a make-shift community center and meeting room. Inside, there was a balding, small-framed white man in his forties clutching a podium. He was addressing about one hundred people, all of whom were sitting at desks and in chairs around him in a sort of horseshoe. There were two levels so that some of the people were a bit higher than others. The crowd featured people from many lands. There were people from Africa, people from Turkey and other Middle Eastern countries. There were Ukrainians and Serbs and Czechs and East Indians. The people seemed agitated and the mayor was working hard to keep them calm and respond to their concerns in a civil manner.

We all took seats and watched. The people were very frustrated—no, angry about the conditions in the projects. The elevators rarely worked, said one woman. An East Indian gentleman complained about the inadequate heat. Another person said it takes forever for the building managers to respond to their needs. Another asked why they couldn't have a decent grocery store in the community.

Again, the similarities to the hundreds of housing meetings I've attended in Chicago were shocking to me. Here I am, thousands of miles and an ocean away from Chicago and people with the least are suffering the exact, I mean exact same insults and mistreatment as those in the ghettos of the United States. Ostensibly to pivot away from the growing discontent in the audience, the mayor began introducing us. Had he known he was about to pour gasoline on the fire, he probably would have had us meet him at his office instead.

He read our brief bios from cards given to him by his aide. After he announced each of our credentials in the struggle, the crowd cheered louder. It was like an announcer reading from an NBA all-star team roster before the big game. Each star's name and stats generating a rising stir among the excited fans. By the time the mayor reached the final name, the crowd was driven to near frenzy. Instead of deflecting the ire, reading our names and our respective roles in the struggle seemed to raise the anticipation and thirst for a fight.

Our presence, and then our credibility as movement warriors, seemed to make the group feel as if they had been joined by the freedom fighter's cavalry, sent specifically to help them in their time of need. To them, we were like legendary social justice samurai replete with scars and mythical heroics from many battles past. Now they would be heard. Now they could demand action. Now they could fight and win.

> **"The philosophers have only interpreted the world, in various ways. The point, however, is to change it."**
>
> Karl Marx

We were swept up. Each of us took turns attacking and recalling history and demanding. By the time we finished, the mayor was forced to make several promises. They had won this battle and we were cheered. The mayor left and didn't ask us to join him. So much for protocol. We were mobbed and spent a great deal of time mingling with the crowd. They knew of Harold Washington. They could recite Malcolm. They had been admirers of our courage and morality in struggle. We were the living manifestation of all the brave souls who had fought against impossible odds and conditions and achieved righteous victory. I learned in that episode that our struggle in the United States has been studied and replicated and admired by people from places farther away than I could have imagined. The world has been watching. Revolution does not need to be televised. The people already know. We experienced the furious reverberation of freedom's struggle in a tiny community center in the suburbs of Amsterdam. It was this moment that seeded the idea for this book.

Can the reverberations be heard back at home?

As African Americans lurch into the twenty-first century we find ourselves grappling with many of the same challenges we have been struggling to overcome for four hundred years. Staggering inequality in wealth and education, media representation (news, not TV), business development, governance at every level, health and well-being, the criminal justice system, and virtually every other significant indicator, continues to plague us. Over the last century, our struggle to even the playing field appeared to give us a righteous sense of morality – of fighting for what is right for all people – and the world paid attention and seemed to generally admire our collective courage and fortitude in the face of withering structural racism. They have even taken note of some of our hard-won victories.

Over that same period, other groups who have also suffered historic injustice such as certain immigrants, women, and the LGTBQ community have benefited from our model of agitation and tireless struggle. They have used our playbook to achieve startling, culture shifting gains. Unfortunately, our own community seems to have abandoned the rules of engagement we invented and now seems to be stumbling aimlessly about. Despite the recent upsurge of Black Lives Matter and outspoken outrage at our condition, we appear to be in a state of suspended animation. We aren't making gains in the areas that matter. In the meantime, other groups using our model surge ahead. What happened? What should we do now? While there is no shortage of noted African American scholars and social commentators weighing in on these questions—few of whom offer interesting or practicable solutions and analysis—the frightening disparities in our communities continue to mount.

Ordinary people in our community under the age of thirty are unimpressed with tales of the 'movement' because their world is harsher and more complex, and they don't see any tangible evidence that those from the civil rights struggle actually helped this anxious generation to succeed—albeit in a shallow, material context. The history and narrative of collective struggle to achieve change no longer seems as appealing to a growing swath of our people. Marches and protests and moral indignation move the community less and less.

The legacy of struggle, the great many stories of breathless courage, the calls to action for the sake of the collective, are losing the psychological battle against the constant corporate refrain of acquiring personal wealth as the only useful measure of one's human worth. Despite the historic fact that our only realistic and successful weapon to overturn our condition has been collective, relentless struggle, we no longer appear to adhere to our own playbook. Sadly, most of us don't even acknowledge the playbook. We have stopped listening to each other, much less fighting for each other, teaching each other, spending our money on each other, loving each other.

Under the circumstances, perhaps it is time for us to listen to others who have watched us for the last hundred years and begin to think about what we project to the outside world and what the world says about us.   It's like when we were kids, and the people close to us tried to tell us some important lesson or truth over and over; but we didn't hear it until that crazy relative said the same thing to us, but this time it was a revelation.

One of our dear friends from Kenya put it very well. He said that African Americans and Native Americans are the only groups in this country that can speak with authenticity about fairness and equal treatment to other human beings, actual democracy, and actual justice, because their leaders spoke of these ideas as their people were being brutalized and marginalized. Each word of the soaring language that led to the governing of this country were written, in large part, by men who enslaved other men and who held great wealth and property. This paradox of liberty runs throughout the narrative and history of this country. Shame on you Cuba, shame on you Russia, shame on you China, say these men, for abuses to your citizens. The world says yes, but what do you say America, about your slavery, your genocide, and the subtle continuation of your Jim Crow laws and unequal systems? There is a rush to buy more weapons to arm oneself against the criminality and savagery of the "those people." Or there is silence. Back to our regularly scheduled programming, says the voice over.

We hope this book speaks with even greater clarity on this issue. We hope it represents a snapshot of what people from places far away have learned from us and how they believe we should renew our march to victory—and how it links to theirs.

This book is a compilation of reflections, interview responses and essays from a variety of noted scholars, authors, thinkers, and activists. We have provided the core questions to give you a context from which to better understand some of what you will read. Interviews followed the basic set of inquiries presented here, but often took off in whatever direction the interviewer found most interesting at the time of the interview. We hope you find their answers and ideas as thought provoking and compelling as we did.

Many of you have developed relationships and had experiences with African Americans in your country, abroad, and/or in the United States. Some of you are from this country and have spent time abroad working with peoples from other lands. Please reflect on and reply to the prompt questions through these lenses.

Questions:

1. What first brought you in contact with Black Americans (or people from other countries)? Have the relationships continued? If so, can you give any personal stories or experiences?

2. What would you say is the level-of-interest in Black Americans living outside the U.S. (Asia, Europe, Africa, etc.)? Do you feel Black Americans are socially accepted in these places?

3. How do your colleagues regard African Americans? Can you relate a specific story or experience that can illustrate your opinion?

4. In your country (or outside the U.S. in general) do you believe Black Americans are generally regarded with admiration, disdain, or indifference? Why or why not? Have you ever heard the term "Ugly American" used to refer to a Black American? If yes, can you give an example?

5. Outside the U.S. have opinions about Black Americans changed within the last decade? If so, why?

6. While it is well-recognized the impact Black Americans have had on American culture (arts, literature, music, social justice movements, politics, etc.), what impact (if any) do you feel African Americans have had on culture outside the U.S.? How widely do you feel your view is shared in your home county (or where you live if living abroad)?

7. Are Black American leaders (both present and past) known your country, and if yes, how are they regarded? If you've

lived abroad, how well are African Americans known those countries? Who would you say are the most highly-regarded Black American leaders outside the U.S.?

8. In your opinion, is there a specific moment or period in the past 400 years of African American history that stands out as being uniquely important?

9. Are there one or more African American individuals whose contributions have influenced your own thinking or activities?

This last question requires a bit of background:

This is a pivotal point in modern history as the global political economy is shifting, American hegemony is being challenged, and many nations and cultures once-considered "underdeveloped" are coming to the forefront. While there is no question Black Americans have been vital to the political, economic and social development of the United States from its inception through the 20th century, there is a widespread feel they have lost ground in the 21st century. Going forward Black Americans are at risk of remaining a marginalized minority as racial prejudices and poverty gain ground, and other ethnic groups fight for their share of America's shrinking base-of-resources.

Black Americans have consistently benefitted from relationships and dialogue with other cultures outside the U.S., just as have other cultures have been enrich by their experience with Black Americans.

10. What insights, opinions, or perspectives would you give to African Americans in this uncertain era as they continue the struggle to repel racism, to maintain hard-won gains, and perhaps most importantly, find footage and advancement going forward?

Section I.
FROM THERE

Buzz standing in front of the former EU headquarters in Strasbourg, France.

PHOTO BY DAVID ROBINSON

GERMANY

1. Manfred Strassen

Manfred Stassen was born in 1939 in Trier, Germany, near the home town of Karl Marx. He studied philosophy and comparative literature / history and political science at the universities of Bonn, Germany, Sorbonne, Paris, France, Liverpool, England, and followed the Salzburg Seminar in American studies, in Austria. His extensive academic career has brought him to teach in major universities in different regions of the world, including Johns Hopkins University in Baltimore, Maryland. Dr. Stassen also headed the German Academic Exchange Service (DAAD) offices in Germany, India, and the United States. He has lived outside his home country for most of his life but does not consider himself an ex-patriot.

Saved by Black GIs and He Never Forgot

| On Question 1:

My first contact with Black Americans occurred right after WW II, when they had not as yet withdrawn from the area of the Rhineland where I was born in 1939, and before the French occupation forces took over. They contrasted favorably with their white U.S. counterparts and the latter, because they did not behave as those who had liberated the Germans from the Nazis, but rather, in view of the destruction and misery, openly demonstrated a sense of empathy with the losers of the war and a particular kindness towards children. These contacts, however, were too ephemeral for lasting relationships to develop. Such relationships I have later developed as a young professor of philosophy at Wesleyan University in Connecticut—a campus with a certain importance for the struggle of African Americans in the Civil Rights Movement and during the opposition to the Vietnam War—as well as later, from 1981 to 1990, as Director of the German Academic Exchange Service (DAAD) for North America in New York, when I began working on a number of German American exchange activities with the goal of increasing African American participation. It is from that time that dates my friendship with the editors of this book, Dr. Alice and Buzz Palmer, which has highly influenced my opinion on the African American community in the United States and its values.

| On Question 2:

The level of interest in Black Americans outside of the United States in general has, in my opinion, suffered a dramatic drop ever since the times immediately after WW I and the inter-war years. While that interest may have always been relatively low in Asia—except for the kind of interest that military occupation triggers—and Africa, it had the well-documented highlights in Europe in the fields of culture and sports, later also politically, during the Civil Rights Movement and the Vietnam War, when principles and tactics of grassroots politics, with a high participation and input of African Americans, began to cross the Atlantic. My experience with Latin America is not long or deep enough to comment on the question.

I do not believe that demographically significant numbers of African Americans—with the exception of their share in the American occupation forces in Germany and Japan—have lived in societies abroad that would allow [me] to gauge the level of their social acceptance. In Germany, for all intents and purposes, the majority of them have integrated well. Most avoided the ghettoization of their existence (by living, as they said, "on the economy", instead of "on the compound"). Some married German women, learned the language, and even joined local sports clubs.

| On Question 3:

In Europe, most people who came into contact, however vicariously, with African Americans, primarily in culture and sports, held them in high esteem. In Germany, this was particularly true in the Weimar Republic (1919–1932) and even during the pre-war years of the Nazi rule in Germany, for the boxer Joe Lewis and the sprinter Jesse Owens in the 1930s, when millions of citizens filled the stadiums, despite the strong discouragement of the regime. The same degree of enthusiasm was never triggered again by later athletic stars such as Muhammad Ali, Michael Jordan or Arthur Ashe. By contrast, W. E. B. DuBois' turn of the century stay at the Humboldt University of Berlin and his productive interaction, for both sides, with German social scientists, is today only remembered by a handful of specialists. - In France, the legendary Josephine Baker and Louis Armstrong are idols to this day, and in intellectual and artistic circles, James Baldwin, Richard Wright and Ralph Ellison from earlier times, and Toni Morrison of a more recent vintage, have not been forgotten. I forego comments on the many well-regarded Black American jazz and blues musicians and their lasting impact on Europeans, since Berndt is, by far, the more knowledgeable source.

The only well-regarded political leader of relatively recent memory is Dr. Martin Luther King. The other main protagonists of the Civil Rights Movement and the opposition to the Vietnam War (such as Malcolm X., Jesse Jackson, Al Sharpton, Julian Bond etc.) or important mayors, like Harold Washington, were known only to a relatively small number of militants and sympathizers or scholars of American Studies, but not to a larger public. Condoleezza Rice and Colin Powell were well known, but not well regarded, primarily because of their association with George W. Bush and the lie about the existence of weapons of mass destruction in Iraq. The opinions about Barack Obama in Europe are split. While, in the beginning, many people welcomed the fact that an African American had made it to the presidency, soon other sentiments prevailed: that he has not really changed very much—including the plight of African Americans and the parameters of racism in America, the outrage of Guantánamo, the NSA espionage on allied leaders etc.—and that he was awarded the Nobel Peace Prize undeservedly and prematurely.

▎ On Question 4:

European assessment of African Americans oscillates between admiration—when they, their talents and achievements, particularly abroad, are well known—and indifference, precisely because a widespread lack of knowledge about and experience with them prevails.

▎ On Question 5:

From 2000 to 2015, knowledge, opinion, and esteem of African Americans around the world have not necessarily dropped, but largely disappeared from the relevant screens, because of a lack of their positive and more visible participation in world affairs, as well as of a vision for the future—that could be directly attributed to them—of a multicultural world in which, for the first time in history, minorities might successfully challenge the hegemony of the old elites. I have never studied this, but, again, my hunch is that none of the many "African American newspapers" is present in foreign countries, on newsstands, in train stations or airports. At least, I have, in my extensive travels, never come across a single one. Other minorities around the world (i.e. the Turks in Germany, the North Africans in France etc.) use this form of export of first-hand information and their auto-stereotypes with considerable success.

| On Question 6:

There is a general consensus in Europe that African Americans have had a lasting impact the world over in music, the film industry, and sports. The recent political impact is limited to the decade from 1964 to 1974. Chief justices and union leaders from their ranks and their impact, in the United States, on social justice in general, and labor rights in particular, has not trickled down to other (major) countries.

| On Question 7:

Dr. Martin Luther King

| Question 8:

The American Civil War, with the abolition of slavery, in the mid-nineteenth century, the Harlem Renaissance in the 1920s, and the Civil Rights movement in the 1960s and 1970s.

| On Question 9:

No

| On Question 10:

It is a delusion to think that "this ... era" is more uncertain than others, and that, therefore, African Americans today are more in need of ideas, energy, and allies than before.

There are, as far as I can see, basically two battlegrounds:

On the national level is the arena for the fight against racism and poverty. The Black American community must put its own house in order and primarily fight the causes of its torn family structures and for the protection and furtherance of its talented youth between eighteen and twenty-eight years of age, ubiquitously threatened by extinction in internecine urban wars, white police violence, and the consequences of irrational gun laws. It also means entering into a productive competitiveness, not controversy, with other ethnic minorities, through accepting the challenges of excellence (more quality education!) and hard labor. It is also to be questioned whether the traditional African American reliance on the [black] churches is still to be given preference over the possible creation of new political parties alimented by [secular] African American and immigrant leaders.

On the international level is the sad reality that too few African Americans have a first-hand knowledge or experience of the social and political conditions and practices in foreign countries. They should aggressively seek a stronger participation in foreign cultural, academic, scientific, and labor exchanges. This requires the development of an open mind, a willingness to leave a cozy lifestyle temporarily behind, and to learn foreign languages.

Blaming the racists, the inequality producers—i.e. the capitalist dominance of Wall Street over Main Street—and the potentially unfairly favored, and therefore more successful other ethnic minorities for one's own condition, is necessary, but not sufficient. Winners will, in the end, only be those who pull themselves out of the swamp they may feel to be in by their own hair.

2. Berndt Ostendorf

Berndt Ostendorf is professor emeritus for North American History at the Amerika Institut, Ludwig Maximilians Universität München (professor between 1980 and 2005). He is the author of *Black Literature in White America* (1982) and editor of *Ghettoliteratur* (1983), *Die Vereinigten Staaten von Amerika 2 Vol.* (1992), *Die Multikulturelle Gesellschaft: Modell Amerika?* (1995), *Transnational America: The Fading of Borders in the Western Hemisphere* (2002) and *Iconographies of Power: The Politics and Poetics of Visual Representation* (2003). Areas of interest include the cultural history of immigration; the politics of ethnic difference, multiculturalism and public culture; creolization and circumatlantic diasporas; American popular culture and the culture industry; New Orleans, Louisiana, and American music. He was a founding member of the International Association for the Study of Popular Music, CAAR, and a long-time co-editor of *Popular Music.* He was a board member of the Rat für Migration, a migration policy think tank, from 2000 to 2011.

Driven By an Inarticulate Flight from German Tradition
Responses to Questions

1. *If you are from a country outside the United States, what first brought you into contact with Black Americans? Have the relationships continued? If so, can you relate any personal stories or experiences?*

Age is of supreme importance concerning the first contact experience: I was born in 1940, socialized in post-war West Germany, defined by WWII, the Cold War, Vietnam and Civil Rights. My political education occurred during the fifties and sixties: I was a participant in the sixties revolution which was inspired by African American agendas and agenda setters. In short, I was socialized during a crucial period of black agenda setting after *Brown [Brown v. Board of Education]* until the Civil Rights legislation of the sixties.

How did I come in contact with African American culture? I recall that I was driven by an inarticulate flight from my own German tradition. I wanted to fly over the nets of extended family, parochial school, Catholic church, regional

"Plattdeutsche" culture, and particularly the Nazi old boy networks during the Adenauer years. What was the pull factor? In my case clearly the haunting siren song of African American music and jazz. Digging into deeper memory layers I discover an interest in the adversarial edge in African American music, prompted by our conflict-ridden situation in restoration Adenauer-Germany. At the age of eleven, twelve or thirteen a certain American musical inflection began to catch my attention, because it promised what seemed to me a sense of freedom—with an anti-authoritarian edge. By the mid-fifties I had already graduated to the musical rebels Charles Parker, Bud Powell, Thelonious Monk, Kenny Clarke, and Max Roach and had become a Bebop snob. How did I get there, mentally and emotionally? Now clearly, it is unusual for a white, Catholic altar boy in the boondocks of Northern Germany with the next city (and record store) thirty miles down the road to develop an interest in the music of American blacks, let alone in Bebop. And thereby hangs a tale.

In 1955, I discovered the Voice of America and Willis Conover. I don't think that I can exaggerate the importance of Willis Conover, anchorman of the *Voice of America Jazz Hour* for the promotion of black jazz musicians and for the development of jazz into a global music during the Cold War – or for my own personal growth. Willis Conover created conspiratorial listening communities and jazz diasporas all over the world, but particularly in Central and Eastern Europe and, like Sim Copans in France and Joachim Ernst Berendt in Germany, created the musical wetlands for the growth of American Studies. At the time of his death in 1996 it is estimated that some tens of millions of people all over the world had listened to his program on the Voice of America.

2. *What would you say is the level of interest outside the United States in Black Americans? (Asia, Europe, Africa, Latin and South America, etc.) Do you feel Black Americans are socially accepted in these places?*

The level of interest and the quality of information is relatively low outside the United States W.E.B. Dubois identified the color line as the chief problem of the twentieth century. Next to the Civil Rights movement it was the global spread of African America popular music and jazz in a world dominated by racism. The musical accompaniment of the political struggle inspired a global interest in African Americans and their specific situation. Finally, it is in the area of sports where Black Americans have achieved a level of acceptance. I do not see much difference in the social acceptance of African Americans throughout the world. It was relatively low at most times and in most regions

3. *How do your colleagues, your countrymen, regard African Americans? Is there a story or incident you recall to illustrate your opinion?*

After WWII black soldiers were perceived by us youngsters both as victors and as victims of the victors. Their balancing act between European acceptance or musical achievement and American racist ascription was quickly noticed and understood by their fans. To their own surprise, many Black musicians—say, Charlie Parker or Miles Davis—served as a role model for European jazz musicians and their young fans. Whereas in European jazz clubs, the color line became increasingly more perforated, it remained firmly in place within the military ghetto.

This situation radicalized the transatlantic double consciousness of African American servicemen. As American citizens and soldiers they remained in the prison house of American racism, while as jazz musicians they enjoyed near universal acceptance and cult status by their fans in Europe. Miles Davis is eloquent about this in his autobiography. At the same time, their musical talent, so strongly appreciated by the European young, remained unacknowledged or grudgingly acknowledged by the white American musical power structure.

The special care accorded to Black American jazz artists by Europeans at first caused some consternation, and it took a while before the State Department recognized their value as a sonic weapon in the Cold War. Reinhold Wagnleitner puts it in a nutshell: "jazz, rock 'n' roll, and Hollywood did not need U.S. cultural propaganda as desperately as U.S. cultural propaganda needed jazz, rock 'n' roll and Hollywood."

4. *In your country – or outside the United States generally – how do you think Black Americans are regarded? With admiration? Disdain? Indifference? Why?*

During the late forties American music came back to Europe within the political frame of occupation, reeducation, and the Cold War. Though Americans had come as victors after both wars, in 1945 the collapse of German culture was so complete that it lacked any authority—particularly for its young: it had abgedankt (i.e., abdicated). This created what is known as the "skeptical generation" whose slogan was: Do not take anything for granted. On the micro-social level of everyday praxis, American democracy entered as a "swinging" democracy. As children we noticed how differently the Black G.I.s dressed, danced, walked, and talked. As a young tot, I made friends with a Black American mess sergeant who traded ditties with me and taught me how to dance. The liberating motor behavior of the American jazz culture signified, when adopted by German jazz fans, a tacit political statement. Who had hated jazz? Victorians, the Nazis, the conservative restoration in Germany, J. Edgar Hoover, Stalin, the Klan, and Fundamentalist religions. The choice was clear.

Let me briefly summarize a generational conflict that this "bastard" of American culture helped to radicalize. It helped that the old anti-communism of the Nazis translated smoothly into the new anti-communism of the Cold War, making instant Cold War democrats out of many a devout Nazi. As a consequence of the ideological vacuum, this older generation opted for a pragmatic and at times cynical acceptance of Western democracy as a, comparatively speaking, lesser evil. Yet, while this group – born before 1920– grudgingly accepted American politics, this acceptance was accompanied by an almost visceral rejection of all American popular, mass or grassroots culture.

The Nazi indoctrination against American modernist "jazz-culture" as represented by Weimar had enjoyed a wide popular base in the older generation that continued into post-war restoration. "Junge mach die Negermusik aus" was heard in many German homes during the fifties, and this meant all American music, including Jewish music which, as the Nazis had noted earlier, was infected by the "Negro virus." While my dad embraced the Cold War rigidities of John Foster Dulles, the post-war generation of youngsters was marching to a different drummer. We wanted a radical political break with the authoritarian past and had many questions to ask our parents.

Hence we embraced the very modernist African American culture that our parents rejected, and we also began to have doubts about the hidden logic of the Cold War that framed our parents' world. So it was the Cold War, Civil Rights, and the Nazi Past (Vergangenheitsbewältigung or "coming to terms with the past") that crisscrossed in the West German acceptance of a Black-inspired American culture and fused into a powerful blend. (The end of the Cold War changed the global scene and the impact of Black politics.)

5. *Do you think opinions about African Americans have changed-for better or worse-over the last decade, for example? If so, why?*

The successful Civil Rights struggle which led to affirmative action, more social justice and political rights had a collateral effect: a growing academization of the protest movement, which shifted from the streets into English departments, e.g. Skip Gates at Harvard. While during the sixties Black America was exclusively on the public radar, other minorities appeared after the seventies, and wanted a piece of the cake. Multiculturalism and diversity reduced the visibility and impact of black politics. We witnessed a growing multilateralization of minority rights. Gerrymandering has led to political gridlock. This needs to be addressed.

6. and 7. *Are Black American leaders (present and past) known in your country or in the country where you lived as an ex-pat? Who are the most highly regarded Black American leaders outside the United States?*

Outside the U.S. the impact of African Americans has been most prominent in popular culture and sports, and much less in politics, with the exception of the years 1965 to1974. Apart from Barack Obama few active and current black politicians are known to the average German newspaper reader. African American newspapers are generally not available (though the white press is). There is respect for W.E.B. DuBois (who had a special relationship with academic Germany) and for MLK and Malcolm X. There is appreciation of black writers, actors and musicians, particularly in the popular media and sports.

We need to differentiate between the various global and regional audiences and between the general public, the educated newspaper readers, academic cohorts. The academic interest in African Americana was particularly strong in Germany during the sixties and after. But the student interest has steadily declined during the past decades. At the same time Afro-Germans have become more visible and Afro-German studies are on demand often in conjunction with Africana studies. The increasing presence of African asylum seekers helped to shift the focus of public interest to African blacks and to the consequences of migration and integration.

6. *In your opinion, and to the extent that you have knowledge, is there a period or a moment in African American history that stands out as being uniquely important?*

The Civil War, Tin Pan Alley, the Harlem Renaissance, sports (Joe Louis, Jesse Owens, Muhammad Ali).

Clearly the Civil Rights movement and anti-Vietnam struggle with its charismatic leaders Martin Luther King and Malcolm X are landmarks of American history.

7. *Are there one or more African Americans who have influenced your thinking and work? If so, how and why?*

Frederick Douglass, W.E.B. DuBois, Ralph Ellison, James Baldwin, Amiri Baraka, Orlando Patterson, Zora Neale Hurston, Toni Morrison, Thurgood Marshall, Charlie Parker, Dizzy Gillespie, John Coltrane, Miles Davis, Thelonious Monk, Sarah Vaughan, Billie Holiday and Lester Young, Duke Ellington and B.B. King.

This last question requires a bit of background

Black Americans have consistently benefitted from associations and dialogues with peoples and cultures outside the United States. Michel Fabre, in his book **From Harlem to Paris,** *talks about African Americans who went to Paris right after slavery and long before the iconic Harlem Renaissance Period and before World War I to seek ideas and relationships. Black soldiers in World War II, and to some extent in subsequent wars and postings outside the U.S., returned home with broader world views. Dr. King went to India and affirmed non-violence. The list goes on.*

Scholars are saying this is a pivotal point, an axial period, when, for example, American hegemony is being challenged and many countries heretofore labeled "underdeveloped" are coming to the forefront. While it is documented that African Americans have been part of the warp and weave of America's political economy and social development from its beginnings through the 20th century, there appears to be a feeling among some that Black Americans are losing ground in the 21st century. That Black Americans may be at risk of becoming a marginalized minority as racism and poverty gain ground, as the nature of work and well-being changes, as new alignments take shape, and as other ethnic Americans compete for resources, recognition, and their places at the tables of influence.

8. *What insights, opinions, and/or perspectives would you give to African Americans in this uncertain era as they continue to struggle to repel racism, to maintain hard-won gains, and, perhaps most importantly, to find footing and advancement nationally and internationally going forward?*

- Avoid political parochialism (e.g. a racial tunnel vision)

- Form alliances with other discriminated minorities in the United States

- Support protest movements at home: prison industrial complex, racial profiling, politics of redistribution, gun control, global warming

- Get involved in American foreign policy: combine postnational, postcolonial and postracial agendas

- Form international alliances, particularly with Africa, the Caribbean and South America

- Shift the focus from issues of race to issues of class (on the basis of new domestic alliances)

- Fight the corrupting influence of normalcy: deconstruct deep-seated racial habits of the heart

UNITED KINGDOM

Buzz meets with John Hume who brokered the peace deal between the British and the IRA. They are joined by MP Glynn Ford at the EU headquarters in Strasbourg.

1. Glynn Ford

In 1999, Glynn Ford was elected as a member of the European Parliament for the constituency of South West England for both the Labor Party and the Gibraltar Socialist Labor Party, holding the seat for two terms after being re-elected in 2004. He was also Chair of the European Parliament's Committee of Inquiry into The Growth of Racism and Fascism in Europe (1984–86) and rapporteur for a second European Parliament Committee of Inquiry into Racism and Xenophobia. He served as the European Parliament's representative on the Council of Ministers Consultative Commission on Racism and Xenophobia (1994–99).

Black Thinking Resonates with My Thinking

For a variety of political reasons, I have been active for thirty years in UK and Europe in the anti-fascist and anti-racism struggle. I became politically active in Britain during the brief heyday of the National Front (NF) in the 1970s and I became a Local Councilor in East Manchester where the Tory Council allowed the NF to rent the local town hall. To stop that we used both the streets and the ballot box. We organized mass demonstrations to block access to the buildings and put on the election address of all Labor candidates a commitment that if elected we would ban them from municipal premises. I was elected to the European Parliament (EP) in 1984. Simultaneously ten members of the French extreme right Front National led then by Jean-Marie Le Pen—and now by his daughter Marine Le Pen—arrived in the EP. Le Pen formed a fascist group in the EP with the neo-fascist Italians and a Greek. The left responded by setting up an official Committee of Inquiry into the Rise of Fascism and Racism in Europe and I was elected as its Chair. In 1989 we followed up with a second Committee of Inquiry on Racism and Xenophobia where I was responsible for drafting its report. Subsequently I was elected Treasurer of the Anti-Nazi League in the UK and still serve on the Steering Committee of its successor organization, Unite Against Fascism. I also was appointed for four years to the Council of Ministries Consultative Committee on Racism and Xenophobia that recommended both the establishment of an Anti-Racism Observatory (RAXEN) and an EU Anti-Racial Discrimination Directive. All of this inevitably meant I had extensive contact with Black communities across the European Union (EU).

I first met Buzz at an anti-racism conference in Manchester in the early nineties. Following that initial introduction, I spoke at a number of venues in the U.S. with the help of Buzz and Alice: in Chicago—on a platform with Bernie Sanders' wife—in Washington at Howard University and New York on a number of occasions, many as part of the Transatlantic Conference on Race and Xenophobia. I also got to meet with the Congressional Black Caucus (CBC) collectively and individually. I met Carol Moseley-Braun, Bobby Rush and Danny Davis in Chicago and many others in Washington and Brussels including Barbara Lee and Alcee Hastings. I used these CBC contacts to try to pressure the U.S. administration over Diego Garcia. Britain had expelled all the inhabitants of the Chagos Archipelago—now called the British Indian Ocean Territory—of which Diego Garcia is a small part. There is a campaign to allow them to return, at least to the other islands in the archipelago, and the United States publicly acknowledging its support would be invaluable. It is no security risk.

When I first went to Chicago to meet up with Buzz and Alice I soon saw for myself just quite how segregated a city it was. When I flagged down a cab in the center and gave the (white) driver their address he said, "You've got to be joking. I haven't been down there in two years." Another time a white professor who volunteered to drive me to their home for a dinner party got increasingly nervous the further south we went, locked the car doors and muttered, "It's a long way."

I come from the European Social Democrat tradition with the mindset that goes with it. The thinking of the Black American community resonates better with me than any other demographic constituency in the United States. White Americans are generally on a different page. Some are even reading a different book.

I also in a different aspect of my work spend a lot of time in East Asia. Asians tend to be quite racist. Black African Americans are grudgingly accepted at best in my opinion. This is anecdotal rather than any sophisticated analysis. There have been exceptions. I sent Buzz a book (The East is Black) about the strong links between African Americans and the Chinese Communist Party in the seventies, and I'm just reading Eldridge Cleaver's book—*Juche*—that contributed to the thinking of the Black Panthers.

Most Europeans don't know any African Americans and their perceptions are shaped by the unflattering pictures draw by the TV, films and what they read in the newspapers. There is a continuing low-level dialogue with the EP's Anti-racist Group and the Congressional Black Caucus. We have certainly until recently had two-day annual meetings often around the German Marshall Fund's annual conference in Brussels. The more contact the better. We were exploring the idea of specifically recruiting Afro-American and Asian American interns for MEPs in Brussels and ensuring that amongst the EU centers paid for by the European Commission there are some based in black colleges and universities.

In Europe, political progress is driven by campaigning and struggle. Women didn't get the vote because some politician woke up one morning and thought it would be a good idea. Nor will minority communities get their rights without being out on the streets as well as active in the ballot box. Yes, there has been progress, but there is still a long road ahead.

The recognition of Black Americans is media driven. Outside of film stars it's Obama, Colin Powell, Jesse Jackson, Martin Luther King. It's the Civil War and Civil Rights struggle that is black history for Europeans. These were major turning points. For me one of my greatest honors was to spend two days escorting Nelson Mandela around the European Parliament when he was a guest of the Socialist Group.

Situations are transformed. Initially the Centre Right in the EP strongly resisted my report. In Committee it scraped through with a minority opinion signed by all the opposition. Now its conclusions are largely commonplace. Yet sometimes we can be our own worst enemy. The progressive members of the Committee of Inquiry agreed we had to focus and we agreed to look for a dozen or so recommendations. The problem was when it came to the crunch everyone wanted a different dozen; consequently, the final report ended with 108 recommendations. But the price of progress is eternal vigilance. The RAXEN Center in Austria set around 2000 [recommendations] after the work of the Council's Consultative Commission finished its work in 1999 was subsequently diluted out of existence by the powers that be. They killed it with kindness. With no additional staff or resources, its geographical and political mandate was enlarged to the point where it was no longer capable of doing the in-depth work needed.

In conclusion I would say agitate, organize, legislate. We need the intellectual underpinning as ammunition, but what fires progress is people on the street and in the polling booths. "Our Agenda, Not Theirs" happens when we make it.

2. Lord Meghnad Desai

Currently, Lord Meghnad Desai is chairman of the Official Monetary and Financial Institutions Forum (OMFIF) Advisory Board, an independent membership-driven research network. Previously, he has worked as an Associate Specialist in the Department of Agricultural Economics, University of California, Berkeley, and was professor emeritus at London School of Economics, where he founded the Centre for the Study of Global Governance. Desai has written extensively publishing over 200 articles in academic journals and a series of books.

And So Sayeth the Lord

Let me start with my background. I was born in Baroda, a town in Gujarat in Western India. I spent my first ten years there and then the next eleven in Bombay (now Mumbai). I did my BA and MA in the University of Bombay and in 1961 I got a Ford Foundation Fellowship to study for PhD at the University of Pennsylvania. After finishing my PhD in 1963, I spent two years working at the University of California, Berkeley. I left the United States in mid-1965 and came to London to teach at the London School of Economics. I have lived in London for the past fifty years. I married an English woman in 1970, had three children, and separated after twenty-five years. I married an Indian woman in 2004. I live in UK, having retired after forty years teaching at LSE, and am a member of the House of Lords. I have travelled many times to the USA since leaving in 1965, taught summer school twice at the University of Wisconsin, Madison, and been a consultant with the UNDP [United Nations Development Programme] on the Human Development Program.

I became aware of Black Americans quite early in my childhood as I was a precocious reader. We were made aware of the novel *Uncle Tom's Cabin* by Harriet Beecher Stowe. I saw my relations reading *Gone With the Wind,* though I did not. We saw Hollywood movies which had some Black Americans—westerns and Tarzan films. I was aware of Lincoln and the U.S. Civil War. We used to read comics [with] some illustrated Black American characters.

As Communism was quite popular, we had heard of Paul Robeson as a leading black singer and Left activist. We had also heard of Dr. Ralph Bunche. Even so, our awareness of Black Americans was sparse. Indians of my high caste background thought of themselves as fair skinned and not black. They were also the elite in the social and ritual hierarchy. They would identify blackness with inferior status. We were aware that other Indians—especially in the South of India—were darker than us Western Indians.

I recall reading the review of a novel, probably originally in German, but translated in English. It was about a German family which had volunteered to be a host family for American GI stationed in Germany and being shocked when a Black American turned up.

When I was about to go abroad, my mother was worried that I would go and marry a white woman—a white ghost as she described. So, I said jokingly, "OK, I will marry a black woman". She was doubly horrified as she had never quite known that there were Black Americans. She did not want me to marry any American woman—white or black.

We had read about President Eisenhower ordering national guards to [accompany] James Meredith into the University of Mississippi. So, we knew about the racial discrimination.

On the other hand, we were aware of Black Africans. As a recently independent colony, India was supportive of the independence movements in Africa, especially the countries under British rule. Kwame Nkrumah had visited India and I recall cheering his motorcade as it went through the streets of Bombay. We had also been proud of Nehru's role in the Afro Asian Summit at Bandung, where many African leaders had gone. We had heard of Kenyatta, Nyerere and Kaunda. I had read about apartheid and Dr. [D.F.] Malan who was Prime Minister of South Africa.

During my first year in college, one of our texts was Mahatma Gandhi's account of his Satyagraha in South Africa. That recounted the story of racial discrimination in South Africa, as well as his account of his role during the Zulu rebellion.

During my two years in the master's degree [program] at Bombay, we had two African students. One was from Ghana, Kobina Onumah, who was in my year; and one from Nigeria, whose last name was Nalilungwe, who was one year my junior.

Arriving in Philadelphia, I became aware of the presence of Black Americans. The campus was located not far from the Black residential areas across Market Street just beyond 40th [Street]. I was always an avid book reader, so soon I came across the works of W. E. B. Dubois. I also read the novel Go Tell It on the Mountain by James Baldwin. That gave me an insight into the lives of Black Americans.

There were few graduate students who were Black Americans at Penn. We had, however, a faculty member who was Black American. Andrew Brimmer was teaching money and banking. Lyndon Johnson chose him to be the first Black American on the Federal Reserve Board. This happened after I had left Penn in July 1963, but made me very happy.

I guess the contact with Black Americans was as waiters and waitresses. Going around Philadelphia, I saw many Black Americans, but did not get to talk to anyone that I can recall. I was not at all prejudiced or put off. But there was no normal channel of meeting Black Americans. I did once attend a drumming session in a hall on the ghetto side of Philadelphia and wanted to know more but did not pursue it.

The Civil Rights movement had begun by then. I was aware of the NAACP. There was not much action at Penn while I was there (until mid-1963). I do remember thinking that President Kennedy was not as vigorous in pursuing civil rights legislation as he could be. There was a report of a meeting Bobby Kennedy had with Black civil rights activists when the black delegation walked out, as they were dissatisfied with the lack of commitment—in part—of the Kennedy administration. If my memory is right this was in the early part of 1963. I read about it in NYT [*New York Times*].

It was when I got to Berkeley that I became more aware of the Civil Rights movement. The summer of 1963 had witnessed the murders of the students who had gone South. There were also beginnings of the movements in Birmingham, Alabama. I became aware of Dr. Martin Luther King and his work. But the Urban League was another organization we got to know of. We were aware of not saying Negro but Afro- Americans. The ferment for equality in hiring and other civil rights were being discussed in newspapers. I took part in a couple of pickets outside supermarkets, carrying placards about hiring black workers. Once, we had a massive demonstration outside a seafood restaurant in Oakland where Senator Knowles came to support the owner who refused to hire Black workers. It was a matter of great pride for us to confront the police peacefully. At the end we all linked arms and sang, We Shall Overcome".

By 1964, the issues of civil rights and [the] Vietnam War were coming together. In Berkeley we had the Free Speech Movement (FSM) which arose out of students who had been arrested for civil rights activity and faced suspension on campus. This double jeopardy was the beginning of FSM. I was on the academic staff at Berkeley, not a student; but I was supportive and stood bail bond for many students in 1965 when they were getting arrested for the anti-Vietnam War movement.

I followed the debates about Lyndon Johnson's civil rights legislation. Given how badly Johnson was portrayed when he was vice president by the Kennedy people and also after he became president, it was heartening to see him achieve the passage [of civil rights legislation]. I was also there when Dr. King was awarded the Nobel Prize. I read about the March on Washington D.C. and his great speech and also his murder soon after. By this time, I was in the UK.

Let me now come to some other questions. In India there is awareness of Black Americans. The political leadership of all parties have been supportive of the Black Americans. The people of India are supportive from a distance but I have encountered a lot of prejudice against black people among the Indian diaspora in UK and the United States. In India, there are stories of prejudice against Nigerians. Formally, Indians are free of color prejudice; but in real life, I am less sure.

In the UK, where I have lived for fifty years, the situation is very different. Soon after I arrived we had the racialist speech by Enoch Powell MP and I organized a teach-in against it at LSE. But in the years since then there has been a genuinely multi-racial society created here. These are people from African and Caribbean countries and the 'Asians' are from the Indian subcontinent or Sri Lanka. There [are] MPs who are Black and Ethnic Minority (BME), as well as in local authorities. There is always more to be done but there is progress in the fifty years. As far as Black Americans are concerned, people are aware of Malcolm X, Dr. Martin Luther King. They are aware of the singers and performers, though not of many Black writers.

3. Florence Kabba

Dr. Florence Kabba was born and raised in the UK, and has lived in West Africa, Switzerland and the United States. She is an associate professor in the Department of Education and Language Acquisition at LaGuardia Community College, CUNY, New York. She received a bachelor's degree in humanities at Greenwich University, England, and an MS in politics at the London School of Economics, England. She also has an MA in TESOL from Hunter College, New York, and a doctorate in English education from Teachers College, Columbia University, New York. Dr. Kabba has presented papers at conferences and written on issues related to diversity in teacher training, black book club reading practices, and the intersections of race, gender, language and critical literacy.

African Americans Have a Certain Power

I came into contact with African Americans when I came with my ex-husband to live and work in New York in 1984. Since being here I have made friends with African Americans and have colleagues who are African American.

I think that in the UK, the Caribbean, and most of Africa, there is a great deal of interest in African Americans. Even before President Obama was elected there was a sense that African Americans have a certain power, an ability to make white society listen to their demands and act on it. From my perspective as someone born in the fifties and raised in England, this belief in the agency of African Americans stems from the civil rights era when we saw on our television screens African Americans, headed by Dr. Martin Luther King, unite to make changes in American society and dismantle segregation. Malcolm X was an additional guiding influence and a source of pride because of his insistence that blacks had a right to self-defense and self-determination. There was also during the Black Power movement in the seventies among my peers and my family a respect for the "audacity" of African Americans to say that they were "black and proud" and to proclaim this loudly and unapologetically through leaders and organizations, such as Stokely Carmichael and the Black Panther Party. It seemed to us then that African Americans were fearless in a way that we in England weren't. We faced racial discrimination, but we did not have the numbers or a strong enough sense of a shared history to come together and fight for our rights as effectively as blacks in America were able to. Therefore, we looked to African Americans for inspiration and guidance on how to conduct our own struggles. In the sixties and seventies blacks in the UK did attempt to organize. There were several black organizations, such as the Black United and Freedom Party (BUFP), which styled itself on the Black Panther Party. Additionally, we organized Saturday schools. For example, the Marcus Garvey School, which I was a member of, was founded by Peter Moses to support the literacy skills of black school children, who were starting to be labeled as "educationally subnormal." An important mission of these Saturday schools was also to provide black children with knowledge about their historical past and teach them aspects of black history that were and are still being left out of the school curriculum. Clearly all of this demonstrates the level of interest in African Americans and the influence that they have exerted over blacks in the UK.

I think that there is an ambivalence towards African Americans. On the one hand, there is a respect and admiration for the courage and determination African Americans have in fighting for their rights. The Black Lives Matter movement is a case in point. Many of us wish that we could make white society listen to us the way that African Americans have forced white society to listen to them. Also, African American artistic expression is admired. In Europe we are heavily influenced by African American music, style and literature. On the other hand, there seems to be a loss in their sense of self-worth.

While there is still a respect for the ability of African Americans to unite and to refuse to accept unequal treatment, I think there has been a shift in perceptions of them. I believe that to a large degree white Americans love African American culture, but they don't much like African Americans. Consequently, American society has modified and commodified black culture without truly recognizing African Americans as being equal. This appropriation of black culture has created an illusion of acceptance that has led African Americans to surrender much of the values that have allowed them to persevere as a people. I think that African Americans have bought into the "American Dream" and are considered in many ways to be trying too hard to assimilate into white mainstream culture. There exists today a materialism that seems to function as the bottom line, and this is seen as resulting in a lack of dignity. For example, reality shows and talk shows display African Americans as immoral, "out there" and "ignorant." This perception did not exist before.

As noted above, African Americans have had a huge political impact on black people in the UK. However, I believe that the political influence was stronger in the past and therefore younger people today—those in their twenties and thirties—have less knowledge about the political sphere of influence. I think that there has also been a strong cultural influence on the majority of Black British people. Sports figures, from Muhammad Ali to Venus and Serena Williams, are considered standard bearers for their skill, grace and excellence. Writers like James Baldwin, Toni Morrison and Maya Angelou are respected not just because of their literary skills, but because they write or wrote about black people in all their dimensions and therefore have helped question stereotypes and create a sense of pride for all black people—not just African Americans. Musicians from the early soul singers like Aretha Franklin to rap super stars like Jay Z are admired for the ways in which they produce music that speaks to the heart and soul of the lived black experience. I think, in particular for black British youth, rap speaks to the frustration and aspirations of a people who are marginalized and powerless. At the same time, it's a double-edged sword because I think for some, rap is seen as embedded in African Americans' embrace of materialism and their loss of values.

I'm not sure what current political figures the average black British person is familiar with. Barack Obama is an obvious choice. Among my peers his election was considered a victory not just for African Americans but also for all of us. Also, when I was in the UK in 2015 I read a brief article about a black family whose son was either killed or injured by whites or the police (not Stephen Lawrence) and that they were being stymied in their efforts to bring the perpetrators to justice. What struck me most upon reading the article was that they had been in contact with Al Sharpton's Action Network to get advice on how to proceed. There is some awareness of the Black Lives Matter movement, although I'm not sure how widespread it is. Past leaders that some might know of could be Dubois, and definitely Malcolm X.

Toni Morrison really influenced me. Firstly, her skill as a writer captivated me because I have always been an avid reader and nursed an ambition to write from an early age. However, it was the stories she told, which spoke not only to the self-denigration that is almost inescapable when one lives in a society rampant with racism, but also to the beauty of black people and black cultures. To find this expressed in artistic form in a manner that was accessible to me has probably made her the biggest influence on my thinking and on my work.

I think there is a lot of important political work being done in the country to fight oppression. I'm thinking in particular of the Black Lives Matter movement, but the international connections are not always being made. As you point out, Martin Luther King went to India and gained the strategies that he employed in his philosophy of passive resistance. Dubois made international connections with African nations and was part of the Non-Aligned Movement. Malcolm X took the case of African American subjugation to the United Nations. However, today I sense a bit of a retreat, a hunkering down so that the struggles that African Americans engage in become viewed as localized and particularistic rather than global. I think that to have an impact on the world that would lead to the advancement of African Americans and other black peoples, African Americans have to do several things. First, I think that African Americans have to recapture a greater sense of self-worth as a people and refocus on the spiritual values that not only helped them survive, but helped maintain their connections with other black people across the globe. Secondly, I think this will facilitate their ability to organize not as a minority, but as representative of a non-white majority in the world.

DENMARK

Peter Plenge

As Aalborg University Director, Peter Plenge was the leader of the University of Copenhagen's Central Administration, including Budget & Accounting, Student Affairs & Records, Human Resources, Leadership Support, Buildings, ICT Systems, Alumni Relations, External Relations, and Patents & Contracts. The university director, president, and vice president form the top leadership of the university.

Northwestern U Professor Jan Carew, Peter Plenge, Buzz Palmer meeting with Mayor Harold Washington.

"They're Denmark-bound"

So read the headline of a piece in *The Daily Calumet* newspaper of mid-August 1989. The traveling party included five students and two teachers from Olive-Harvey College, one of the seven Chicago City Colleges. The students had been chosen from among students from Olive-Harvey's Architectural Technology program. In Denmark, the group was to participate in a new semester-long exchange program, the "Urban Renewal and Ecology Technology Program" (URET), organized and co-sponsored by Olive-Harvey College and Aalborg University. During the fall semester 1989, the students would, together with Danish students, work on a study project on energy conservation and recycling technology. Besides educating the students, the program would also contribute input to the urban planning authorities in Chicago on resource recovery and sustainable development of a former steel mill site in southeast Chicago.

Three of the students had an African American background, two a Hispanic. They came from working-class families. When young people from their neighborhoods went abroad, it was more often as members of a U.S. military force (Olive-Harvey being a good example) than as scholars. But this trip was a learning mission.

The goal was to show that education was a marvelous means to build bridges between people from different parts of the world and to solve common problems through intellectual and technical cooperation and knowledge-sharing. However, a number of risks were to be considered in order to ensure that the students got the intended outcome of the program. It could not be taken for granted that a group of minority students from a two-year college in Chicago would fit unproblematically into a Danish (university) environment. In order to get the benefits of the exchange program they should feel safe, confident and motivated enough to follow lectures and participate in group work with their Danish classmates. It was evident that a successful implementation of the program not only depended on the students' own efforts, but also on a conscientious preparation and on-going monitoring of the course of events from the two schools so as to safeguard the students against risks that could derail their studying in Aalborg.

This piece offers details on the basic ideas behind the URET Program, the people who instigated it, and how it proceeded. The initiators of the program were a group of African American Chicagoans and Danish Aalborg citizens who all subscribed to the idea that all young people with the necessary talent, diligence and dedication should have access to higher education, independent of family fortune. In Denmark, education is regarded a citizens' right, not a consumers' right. It is, therefore, financed by the tax income of the Danish state. The political thinking behind this system is that education, like healthcare, defense, the judiciary and police, must be the responsibility of the community. Whereas the market may be an effective means to balance supply and demand and ensure dynamic competition, it is not effective as a means to ensure social cohesion and a fair distribution of opportunities when it comes to education. The URET Program was to increase the Chicago exchange students' chances of getting good jobs and, at the same token, contribute to the development of urban renewal and recovery plans for the southeast side of Chicago. The program should also widen the horizon of the Danish co-students who were engaged in similar problems of replacing old industries in the region of North Jutland by contemporary, sustainable alternatives. Convinced by these perspectives, the leadership of the City Colleges of Chicago and Aalborg University decided to allocate the time and money that it would take to run the URET Program.

The first contacts leading to the program were made at the Whither America Conference arranged by Professor Ib Joergensen and his colleagues at Aalborg University in December 1984. The topic of the conference was the future social and political development of the United States. Among the participants were Professor Jan Carew of Northwestern University and Mr. Edward "Buzz" Palmer, leader of the Black Press Institute in Chicago. Both were prominent members of the intellectual-political African American environment in Chicago. They were acquainted with Rev. Jesse Jackson and contributed among others to the conference with first-hand information on Jesse Jackson's Rainbow Coalition initiative.

In May 1985, in my capacity as Head of Administration at Aalborg University, I attended a conference in Portland, Oregon organized by the Association for Institutional Research (AIR). I subsequently went to Chicago to investigate the possibilities of a collaboration between Chicago universities, in particular Illinois Institute of Technology (IIT) and the University of Illinois at Chicago (UIC), and Aalborg University.

During my visit to Chicago, I was kindly hosted by Professor Jan Carew and his wife Joy G. Carew. I stayed with them in their home in the South Side neighborhood of Chicago for one week. Buzz Palmer and his wife Alice had, together with Jan and Joy Carew, prepared a busy program for me during the visit. Buzz drove me around to the various meeting points acting at the same time as cultural interpreter, political ambassador, and guide. Meetings had been arranged with, among others, Mayor Harold Washington, Senator Richard Newhouse, President Thomas L. Martin of IIT, and President James Stukel of UIC. During my conversations with Jan Carew and Buzz Palmer, the seeds to the URET Program were sowed. Jan Carew was impressed by the Danish Folkehøjskole (people's high school), where people from all strands of society got together in free studies of art, literature, history and political relations. He thought that Chicago and the United States might get a valuable insight in new inclusive pedagogical methods of the Danes. Jan, therefore, suggested that Aalborg University, as a university with a strength in technical science and a global leader in sustainable energy research, host an exchange program on these topics for a group of Chicago students. The experiences obtained by the students in Denmark could later be employed in urban planning projects in southeast Chicago.

After my return to Denmark, I informed the president of Aalborg University, Professor Sven Caspersen, about my discussions with the Chicago colleagues on organizing an exchange program. Sven Caspersen immediately accepted the proposal and commissioned me to proceed with the preparations. As part of the preparatory activities Professor Caspersen visited Chicago in August 1985. He stayed with the Palmer family in their home in the South Side of Chicago. During the visit, Buzz Palmer gave Professor Caspersen the "Grand Tour" of Chicago introducing him to a number of academic and political leaders of the city.

With Sven Caspersen's visit to Chicago, the basic network of decision makers was established and the practical planning of the program could begin. This turned out to be a time-consuming exercise. Joy Carew, who was working at the City-Wide College of Chicago City Colleges, coordinated the development of the initiative on the U.S. side. She deliberated the mission, the content, the institutional placement, as well as organized the funding of the program with the leadership of the CCC, of Olive-Harvey College and external supporters. On the Danish side, Professor Klaus Illum, an expert in wind and bio-mass energy technology, together with colleagues from the Department of Planning and Social Development, developed the syllabus of the program. In February 1988, Klaus Illum and I—together with one of Dr. Illum's colleagues—went to Chicago for a final discussion of the program with Jan and Joy Carew, Buzz and Alice Palmer, President Homer Franklin of Olive-Harvey College and his colleagues, Professor John Ragona and Professor Howard Stanback. Later the same year, the network between Chicago and Aalborg was strengthened and extended through a number of study trips and planning meetings. The initiative got political support from a member of the Illinois State Senate, Senator Richard Newhouse, who visited Aalborg on March 1, 1989 together with Jan and Joy Carew.

The official launching of the URET Program took place at a press conference in Chicago May 5, 1989. Present were, among others, Chancellor of CCC Nelvia M. Brady, President of the CCC Foundation Jim Rottman, Homer Franklin, President of Olive-Harvey College, Joy Carew, Director of Chicago City-Wide College's Resources Development Program, Terry O'Brian, Commissioner, Metropolitan Water Reclamation District and Andrew Barrett, Representative, Illinois Commerce Commission and Member of CCC Foundation. Present were also the students elected for the program: Craig Thomas, Jorge Velasquez, Chris Rivers, Dwayne Thomas and Milton Banos, plus alternates in case of drop out from among the primary group elected: Latricia Wrettia, Albert Rosas and Rilwan Martins.

In a press release from CCC of May 4, 1989, Chancellor Brady commented "At the City Colleges of Chicago we are committed to producing graduates who are fully prepared to meet the changing needs of today's workplace. As co-sponsor of the Urban Renewal and Ecology Technology Program at Aalborg University we are providing students with exposure to new technologies, methods and cultures that prepare them to be prime candidates for business and industry." Joy Carew explained the mission of the URET Program this way: "This program will offer our students special insights into the new and innovative ways with which the Danes are particularly skilled. We are certain that our students will return with skills and a perspective that can help Chicago." The statements corresponded well with Aalborg University's ambition to establish close and cooperative relations with the surrounding society both in research and education. The students, thus, were about to experience a new cross-disciplinary, problem-based way of working in Aalborg that took its departure from the specific problems of their region of Chicago, e.g. the kind of problems the Southeast Chicago Development Council (SEDCOM) was working with.

In Aalborg, the group was matched with a co-group of eight Danish students. Besides discussions and assistance on educational matters, the Danish students would also function as "buddies" to the OHC students, assisting them with advice on how to get along in Denmark and with the Danes. At a four-day, off-campus kick-off course at a camp site near Aalborg, the American and Danish students got an introduction to the semester. The syllabus contained two projects: a four-week initiating project and a ten-week main project. In the projects, the students were to work on the solution of concrete problems. The description of the problems chosen, the theory and methodology used for the analysis of the problems as well as findings, recommendations and evaluation of the group work, were to be documented in written project reports. The program also included courses in International Communication and Understanding and sessions and exercises in written and general English. The technical background knowledge was provided by lectures on Energy and Environment and Basic Science. Finally, the program included field trips and excursions to sites pertaining to the projects.

Professor Illum, together with his colleagues Knud Erik Hansen and Jan Skajaa and Professor John Ragona and Professor Rowland Matteson from Olive-Harvey College, undertook the teaching and supervision of the students. Klaus Illum's wife, Yvonne Illum, organized the culture and language part of the program. The program was evaluated by the Danish faculty after the conclusion of the fall semester. The evaluation report contained a number of critical constructive observations and recommendations for improvements of the program. The most important observation, though, was that the program actually worked. And—in spite of a number of specific inexpediencies—had provided the students valuable new knowledge capital encompassing not only traditional textbook knowledge, but also knowledge on how to use the knowledge to analyze and solve real-world problems. Last, but not least, the program clearly had improved students' self-confidence. They could actually function and cope with the many uncertainties that they had faced when applying for a place in the exchange program.

In an article in the January 6, 1993 edition of The Chronicle of Higher Education, Joy Carew discussed the outcome of the program for the students. The planners could, of course, not predict how students from the tough neighborhood of southeast Chicago would interact with their Danish classmates. This had not been a problem. On the contrary, through telephone conversations with the students and interviews after their return, Joy Carew had learned that the students had got a new, improved self-esteem. The stereotypes and habitual conceptions about the lack of intelligence and ability of young men of color from southeast Chicago that they were used to at home were absent in Denmark. The expectations of the environment in which they studied in Aalborg gave them a new environment in which to play ball. Initially, they were suspicious that the Danes didn't treat them as they were used to being treated in the United States. "As if the Danes didn't take their "blackness" and "Hispanicness" seriously," writes Joy Carew. On the contrary, both groups were working on urban planning problems related to southeast Chicago and therefore the members of the Danish co-group needed to seek information and advice from the Chicago students. When it came to information and data about Chicago and the community concerns related to the project, these visiting students were now the 'experts.'

Upon their return to Chicago, the students, according to Joy Carew, seemed "to walk prouder" and three of the five formed a study group and devoted a third year to preparing to enter four-year institutions—a goal they achieved. I have no information of their later careers, but I know from conversations with them before their departure from Aalborg that they had developed valuable skills during their stay in Aalborg. Therefore, the Chicago urban planning environment, no doubt, got five motivated and enthusiastic students back from Denmark who were well-equipped to take on tasks on urban development in their hometown. The URET Program showed what two groups of like-minded people can accomplish when they push different backgrounds aside and move together. As a side effect, some long-lasting friendships were built in the process of planning and implementing the program.

The world is not the same in 2015 as it was in 1989, the year when the Iron Curtain fell. Denmark still is a relatively homogeneous society. Statistical comparisons made by the Organization of Economic Cooperation and Development (OECD) in

Paris shows that Denmark has the lowest Gini-coefficient, i.e. difference in income between rich and the poor, in the world. The United States is placed high on the OECD scale. According to OECD, a high inequality in access to higher education weakens the accumulation of human capital and, thereby, growth and wealth. If there is a big inequality, there is an underinvestment in education of children from the lowest strata of society. When they grow up, their potential is not fully used, and this impedes productivity and growth. Furthermore, the quality of education for the children of the lowest income groups gets lower, when inequality grows. This also affects the productivity and growth in a negative direction. Last but not least, OECD finds that in countries with high inequalities, there is a higher risk that children from the lowest social class, when growing up, will be placed outside the labor market. This again will have negative effects on productivity and growth.

Seen against the background of the OECD analysis, the URET Program was the right thing to do in order to support economic growth of southeast Chicago. As an extra benefit, the students brought back skills that made it possible for them to contribute to their urban development project that could underpin sustainable solutions to urban planning projects in the city. The exchange program, obviously, also lifted the students' awareness of the world outside Chicago, their self-esteem and their motivation to learn more.

It may be an up-stream fight in America for education as a basic right of all citizens, but it is important to do so in order to ensure what the U.S. Constitution calls "pursuit of happiness", the European Union calls "social cohesion", and OECD calls "equality". As Buzz Palmer puts it: "La Lotta continua!"

Kaarle Nordenstreng

Kaarle Nordenstreng is a Finnish researcher in information science. Nordenstreng's special areas are communication theory, international communication and media ethics. He is widely known at home and abroad as an expert in communication and communication policy. Nordenstreng has also developed journalistic training and communication research in Finland and internationally, especially in developing countries.

Nordenstreng studied psychology and phonetics at the University of Helsinki. He graduated in 1965. In the same year he became both the Press and Media Assistant at the Social University and the Secretary of the Broadcasting and University Research Group.

In 1966, he traveled extensively in the United States, conducting media research and teaching journalism at Southern Illinois University at Carbondale, Illinois. The following year, he returned to Finland, serving as a research expert at the Finnish Broadcasting Corporation's long-term Planning and Research Institute (PTS). In 1969, Nordenstreng earned a doctorate in psychology. In 1971, he became a professor at the University of Tampere, teaching radio and television courses.

Nordenstreng has been a guest professor at several U.S. universities. In 1981, he worked as a UNESCO expert in Tanzania. He served as chairman of the International Organization of Journalists (IOJ) under the guidance of the Soviet Union between 1976 and 1990.

Without Hesitation

In the mid 1980s, Richard Durham, author, radio dramatist, and founding editor of Muhammad Speaks newspaper, with the largest Black readership in the U.S., asked Buzz Palmer, co-chair of the Black Press Institute, to meet Finnish professor Kaarle Nordenstreng, president of the International Organization of Journalists, at the St. Louis airport during his stop over. Co-chair of the Black Press Institute Dr. Alice Palmer and Professor Jan Carew—author, poet, founding chair of Black Studies at Princeton, and black studies professor at Northwestern University—met with Dr.

Nordenstreng and told him about the BPI's intention to expand the world views of Black journalists through their publication, The Black Press Review, and in Black newspapers.

Without hesitation, Nordenstreng handed Carew and Palmer $100. In addition to Richard Durham, he became one of the first financial supporters of the BPI. At one of Nordenstreng's later visits to the U.S., Buzz Palmer said to him that it would be very productive for members of the Black press, led by the BPI, to receive first-hand knowledge of countries in Eastern Europe and the USSR to make their own assessments of these areas. A week later, Nordenstreng sent Palmer a telegram tasking him with organizing a delegation of fifteen Black journalists. Members of the delegation were chosen for their high journalistic standards, for geographical representation, and as part of a mix of Black journalists who worked for Black newspapers and for mainstream media. The delegation visited key cities such as Prague, Moscow, East Berlin and smaller towns, meeting with journalists, officials and NGOs.

The BPI and the IOJ worked on other joint programs. Jan Carew spent time at the IOJ office in Prague while he wrote his book *The Hour Will Strike Again*, the story of the Grenadian revolution. Additionally, the BPI organized exchange programs with USSR journalists and with the Syndicate of Mexican Journalists. The BPI, with assistance from Nordenstreng and the IOJ, arranged for visiting Soviet journalists to meet with Black journalists and NGOs in Atlanta, Chicago and Washington, D.C., and to speak at major universities in Chicago and the D.C. area. The Mexican syndicate hosted a BPI-led delegation for meetings in Mexico City, including one with a former president of Mexico. A planned exchange between Black American and Russian scholars, in cooperation with the Canadian/USA Institute, never materialized as the USSR imploded.

The IOJ-BPI joint programs enabled Black journalists to take their own measures of issues in areas of the world too often dismissed or stereotyped by mainstream Western media and scholars. During one meeting session of the IOJ in Moscow, for example, Alice Palmer and other Western and developing country journalists, visited Patrice Lumumba University, which provided free education primarily in science and engineering to students from developing countries in Africa, Asia and the Middle East to equip them to modernize their countries. Though the equipment and facility would not compare with advanced Western universities, the level of educational rigor was high, and students from villages and small towns who were not likely candidates for scholarships to Western universities were being educated to the benefit of their country's advancement.

How do we Assess the High Noon of the IOJ and its Decline after 1990?

At one of the final meetings of the IOJ in Yemen, opportunistic members of the organization, anticipating its demise, began attempts to transfer IOJ's financial assets to their own organizations. The International Organization of Journalists had significant holdings and was an economic engine in Eastern Europe's economic sub-structure. Particularly ignoble were the French syndicates' efforts. Some members who had been staunch Socialists abandoned long-held beliefs in a rush to emulate Western business model media approaches. The scurrilous attacks on IOJ President Kaarle Nordenstreng were the most heinous of the ending days.

At its height, the IOJ was the only journalist organization that regularly brought together journalists from around the world with different ideological and political interests, from small and large papers and media outlets, to address matters of world interest and those concerning the rights and safety of journalists. At a time when the world has acknowledged its interconnectedness, the gaping void left by the demise of the IOJ is even more deeply troubling as there is no venue now for such broad-based international gatherings. How enlightening it would be to meet regularly with journalists from the BRICS countries (Brazil, Russia, India, China, and South Africa) as that consortium evolves, and with Portugal, Italy and Greece as they struggle with debilitating, destructive economic downturns.

Moreover, the direct connections to organizations such as the Non-Aligned Movement when the IOJ sent representatives to work with people such as the late Archie Singham at the UN have been lost, as well as women's conferences such as the one held outside Moscow that brought together women from anti-apartheid and civil and women's rights organizations that early on recognized the significant roles women must play in all areas.

As the world wades through the troubling morass of antipathies and sharp divisions between rich and poor, racial animosities, anger against immigrants and the buying-up of media and political processes, the IOJ will be sorely missed.

Buzz Palmer and David Robinson bring members of the
Swedish Trade Commission in to visit Harold Washington.

John P. Kraal

John Peter Kraal was born in Amsterdam in 1961. As a young man, Kraal was drafted into the Dutch army, rising to the rank of sergeant. He later studied chemistry and worked in various professions. In 1999, Kraal began a thirteen-year stint with the Dutch Ministry of Public Health, working primarily in information technology and communications. In 2012, Kraal moved to the United States where he married Muthoni Wambu. He then worked briefly for the National Academy of Sciences, before accepting a position with the Dutch Ministry of Defence in Columbia, Maryland. He currently works with the Embassy of the Netherlands in Washington, D.C.

There are Two Americas—but Neither is Black

The first thing that brought me in contact with African Americans was music. Soul music to be exact. I was about thirteen years old, lived in the Netherlands (where I was born and raised), and every Friday afternoon we had our national pop music countdown (the Top 40) on the radio, and the hits of Motown and Philly Sound artists became a very important part of my early teenage life. In hindsight, I also recall the Black Panthers, and even Martin Luther King's assassination; but at that time, I was too young to understand.

There is a lot of interest in African American culture in the Netherlands and in other European countries. African American fashion and music have a tremendous impact. Many people listen to hip hop, R&B, etc., and wear clothes directly from the United States, and/or derived from African American culture. We are exposed to this on a daily basis through radio and TV, and on a regular basis through Hollywood movies.

Referring to what I mentioned earlier about speaking for my countrymen, in general I would say that the Dutch do not really distinguish between African Americans and other Americans. Basically, they are regarded as Americans first, and – if at all – African Americans second. Once is clear that a person of color is an American, he or she will be regarded and treated as an American. I do have to add that the Dutch generally do not have a detailed knowledge of life in America. And this goes for all Europeans. In the Netherlands, most people, for instance, will say that "a Yankee" is synonymous for "an American". Regardless of the part in the United States that person is from. This gives you a bit of an idea how deep their knowledge of the United States goes. So there certainly is a level of ignorance there. Everything the average Dutchman and woman (and European in general) knows about America is based on what they see on TV, and what Hollywood throws at them.

There are basically two views regarding Americans. Again, the Dutch in general do not distinguish between African Americans and other Americans. One opinion is quite negative: Americans are obese, superficial, gun nuts ("Americans are cowboys") who shoot each other left, right and center on a daily basis, they are crazy and are afraid of everything, they glorify violence and love war, they don't know *anything* about other countries, etc., etc.

And one is quite positive: Americans produce great films, useful and interesting inventions, dominate the music world, have a pro-sports culture; America is the cradle of technology (Apple, Microsoft, NASA, Boeing, etc.,), which is really an expression of an underlying admiration.

But of course, as always, the truth lies somewhere in the middle. As I said before: many people in the Netherlands know little about real life in the United States, and their opinions are mainly based on what they see on TV and in the cinema. Quite honestly, most opinions—both the positive and the negative—expose an undeniable level of ignorance. That, however, doesn't just go for the Dutch. I have travelled all over Europe, and I noticed that one will find these misconceptions in every European country. Also, Europeans feel absolutely superior to Americans. And it doesn't matter if it's white Americans or African Americans (or any other group of Americans). The majority of the people in Europe, especially northern and Western Europe feel that America is a 'humbug' country.

The opinion about African Americans has not changed over the last decade. African Americans are not a topic of discussion in the Netherlands. Nor are white Americans (or any other group) for that matter. What people do talk about—and therefore have an opinion about—are individuals. Those are the stars and celebrities they see in the magazines and on TV. As for specifically African American celebrities, people in the Netherlands love them. They admire the African American Hollywood stars, TV celebrities, sports heroes, and rock (or R&B) stars. Just as they love other American stars and celebrities.

Of course they know that there is a whole other African American reality too. One which consists of large numbers of very poor people. Most people in the Netherlands know that there is an "underclass" of poor people in the United States and that a large portion of that underclass consists of African Americans. Unlike many people in the United States though, they blame this on American society (i.e. unregulated capitalism), and on the U.S. government that doesn't want to do anything for this group of people to get out of poverty.

This is an interesting difference with the general American view, because in the United States many people blame the poor for being poor ("they must be stupid or lazy"). 'Institutional racism' and 'White Privilege' are concepts the Dutch have never heard of, so they wouldn't mention that as a reason for the vast numbers of African American poor people.

This is a difficult question to answer. Of course, Dutch people know Martin Luther King Jr., and some may know Malcolm X. They learned about slavery and (fewer people) know about segregation. Details, though, are far less known, and for most people it is very hard (if not impossible) to fathom what it means to have been African American and have lived in the segregated South during the 1950s or so. The term Jim Crow, for instance, doesn't ring a bell (unless perhaps when you're talking to a history teacher). And even for them, 'knowing' is far removed from 'realizing and feeling' what this must have meant for everyday life.

Culture in the Netherlands and other European countries has definitely been influenced by African Americans over the past forty or so years. Social justice and politics in the Netherlands have not been influenced much by the African Americans in the United States, mainly because we have such a different history and social structure than the U.S. has. I would say the general public in the Netherlands—and even in the rest of Europe for that matter—will share this opinion.

Known African American leaders, are Dr. Martin Luther King, and—to a lesser extent—Malcolm X, and Reverend Jesse Jackson. Most highly regarded by the average Dutch person would definitely be MLK. The main reason for that is that pretty much everyone has heard of him. Others, like Rosa Parks, Harriet Tubman, or Frederick Douglass, for instance, are not known by the general public in my country.

I would definitely answer this question with first and foremost the sixties' Civil Rights movement. And of course 1865, when the South was defeated and the abolition of slavery became a fact in this country. Definitely my wife, Muthoni Wambu Kraal, with whom I have had hours and hours of conversations and debates about institutional racism and White Privilege.

But I would also want to mention my good friend Mr. Anthony Young, who grew up in the South in the 1960s and 1970s, and who has explained a lot to me about life during the time when Jim Crow laws were still in place. Anthony also gave me a book (*The Warmth of Other Suns,* by Isabel Wilkerson), which was a jaw-dropping read for me, being a person that grew up in a different part of the world with a different history and different values.

First and foremost I would say to African Americans in order to make a change (fight racism, poverty, and advance in general): "Use your most powerful weapons! Your voice, and your vote!"

Secondly, find your allies. There are many people who share your opinions (who are not African American themselves), but who are allergic to injustice and will do what it takes to fight it. Team up, grow the movement, and make the change this country needs. Let's not forget: if all minorities in this country would join hands, they would be the majority. And finally: seek exposure (publicity) to gain and keep momentum. Nothing is more powerful than the images we see on social media and on TV.

AFRICA

Poster Bishop Tutu is holding -Freeing South Africa, Freeing Ourselves- is from the cover of an issue of New Deliberations, published by Edward and Alice Palmer, and David Robinson

1. Nigeria – Dr. Shaffdeen Amuwo

Shaffdeen Adeniyi Amuwo is a Clinical Associate Professor Emeritus, University of Illinois at Chicago (UIC). He retired in 2004 after serving in several academic and administrative positions including Associate Dean for Students and Alumni Affairs, Associate Dean for Community and Governmental Affairs, and Associate Dean for Urban Health and Diversity Programs. During his tenure at UIC, Dr. Amuwo brought more young people of the Islamic faith who believed in saving lives and preventing illnesses than anyone in the history of the university. He is also credited for securing over $40M in research and training grants. Dr. Amuwo has received numerous awards for his work promoting the development of minority health professionals. Following his initial retirement, Dr. Amuwo returned to UIC to conduct research and pursue grant funding.

In 2015, Dr. Amuwo left the university permanently to pursue his mission to produce and promote Nigerian and African American health professionals with advanced degrees. Today, he devotes much of this time to Nigerian affairs, both in the diaspora and in Lagos State. He currently serves as the Chairman of the Board of Trustees of the Nigerian Islamic Association (Chicago, Illinois). He is also a member of the Board of Trustees of the Light of Islam (Harvey, Illinois), as well as the Lagos State University Governing Council. Dr. Amuwo has served as a consultant for the Center for Disease Control and Prevention for Lagos State Government.

Interview by David Robinson and Alice Palmer in person
Not Motown—But James Brown

Dr. Amuwo: Good morning. My name is Shaffdeen Amuwo, S-H-A-F-F-D-E-E-N. Last name Amuwo, A-M-U-W-O.

David: Perfect. Dr. Amuwo would you please tell us a little bit of your personal background and some of your professional background?

Dr. Amuwo: Okay, first of all I need to thank Senator Alice Palmer for making sure I'm part of this. We've always done many, many things together, many times the things people hear is just minute compared to what you actually do, not only in terms of my leadership with Senator Palmer, but also my leadership with both Mr. Palmer. I've been in Chicago for forty-six years.

David: You are from?

Dr. Amuwo: I was born in Lagos, Nigeria. In fact, I have only lived in Chicago within a two-mile radius of where we are now. I have never left. Once I got in Chicago, and I lived here on 67th Street. I never left. I will go a little bit north, a little bit south, a little bit east, a little anywhere where it won't be west.

David: You feel at home.

Dr. Amuwo: I came here more so as one of those individuals that were being recruited to study in the Communist Russia at that time. I was to study medicine with many of my friends and then somehow, as fate would have it, my brother was here and he convinced me to come here rather than going to Russia where I would have had a full scholarship. I would have had everything that I needed at that time, based on what was being sold to me and others at that time.

I came here and started working. I would get a little money from home sometimes then. I got frustrated [after] about six months. I wanted to go back because I didn't like the idea of going to work. I was working past right there on 29th Street. I didn't like that idea at all. After some time, I just got used it. [Then] I went to UIC. I finished UIC with my BS. I did biological sciences and African American studies.

David: That's an interesting cross-section.

Dr. Amuwo: Yes, but I mean the perspective at that time was also my grandfather was the president of the Nigerian Islamic Association in Lagos. My interest at that time was to look for a way to serve people. You can't serve people if you don't know about them. Because I want[ed] to be a physician, and you take multiple science and research and things. I'm also empowered to be a physician, and I really need[ed] to know how to serve the people that I live with. That was the reason I did African American studies, and I did quite well. When I left [UIC] I went to school of public health where I had my MPH, Masters of Public Health. I went home [to Nigeria] for a few months, then I decided I wasn't going to do medicine. I came back here, and I wanted to do a PhD. I did my PhD in public health. I got very much interested on issues relative to trying to prevent people from getting ill, trying to address issues that I know…

David: Preventative medicine, behavioral.

Dr. Amuwo: Yes, I knew immediately that I'd probably do better in prevention than in medicine because my heart was in trying to prevent rather than trying to cure. I had a good friend. I don't know. Mr. Wagner. Remember Wagner?

Alice: Jim Wagner, yes.

Dr. Amuwo: Jim Wagner. Okay, he was one of the people that convinced me to do public health at that time. He passed about eight, ten years ago. I became quite involved in public health related issues. During my

PhD exercise, I called it, I didn't say I was very smart. I did very well in biostatistics and epidemiology and I was leading a review group at that time. They started a PhD, the new PhD, Doctorate of Public Health. I was one of the first to apply and everyone that was in my group was admitted, but me. Yes, that was the truth, all of the people that actually applied...

David: It must have been a bit of a shock for you, a bit of a...

Dr. Amuwo: Well I live on the South Side. I live among my folks and I know what they go through, so I wasn't really shocked because the people that are living far north in Lincoln Park are the people that will say, "That was unexpected." When they didn't admit me, I tried to look for a way to do my PhD. I contacted somebody who said, "Well you could easily do your PhD taking courses here. We examine your credentials and communicate it." I did my PhD externally. I didn't finish at UIC, but what actually taught me is the fact that if it had to happen to me and I was the person leading the tutorial, what will happen to others who were not doing so well as I was doing? You get what I'm saying?

David: Yes, I get it.

Alice: Yes, I do too.

Dr. Amuwo: Of course, I was already married. I had children. I've only had one wife.

David: That's good.

Alice: That's very good.

Dr. Amuwo: It's been forty years.

David: That alone is something to celebrate.

Dr. Amuwo: Walking down the streets with me.

David: Very good, very good.

Dr. Amuwo: I would say I had a lot of good support from home. But then what I actually learnt is the fact that I needed to do certain things to correct what happened to me, not because I had this idea of what happened to world problems. My dissertation was on sickle cell disease, which the attempt at that time was that people [who] have [the] sickle cell trait are supposedly diseased [and] either were denied insurance coverage or had to pay a lot for insurance. I did my study more so to find out in terms of what people really feel about sickle cell disease, sickle cell traits. All of my subject[s] were from the west side. Annie Jenkins was very helpful. You remember Hart Adams? He just passed last week. Adams were very well helpful. Those are people that impacted my life....

David: Ms. Jenkins was one of my mentors.

Dr. Amuwo: I collected my data most to try to educate the public, and west side communities in terms of difference between sickle cell disease and sickle cell trait. And [to] try to impact on them that sickle cell trait individuals will actually live a normal life all with a sickle cell trait. It was my father and I didn't have any experience relative to my sickle cell trait status, absolutely nothing. But any time people say, "You have sickle cell," which makes it different from, "You have sickle cell trait," that's sickle cells and you have the disease, people with the disease now they're living with [it] much better. That was what my dissertation was all about.

Beyond that what I then did at that time was to now say that I needed to go back to school of public health. Number one during the interim while I was doing my PhD externally which took about four to five years they had not admitted one black person to PhD at [the] school of public health. The record [for] even those who were pursuing masters was abysmal, so as I was going to collect that somehow Mr. Wagner left his job at school of public health and I convinced, you know, Morris Wrap?

Alice: Yes, I remember him.

Dr. Amuwo: Maurice Rabb, the first black ophthalmologist in Illinois. I was working in the middle of great people.

David: Good time, you were coming up at a very good time.

Dr. Amuwo: Dr. Maurice Rabb convinced the dean at that time to hire me. He said, "That's a smart guy. You need to hire him." I was hired to replace Wagner, but we had some other intentions. My intention was to look for a way whereby we can get black people to do public health.

David: Excellent. Now, let me stop you. We're going to come back to that, but I want to reel your life tape back a bit and provide a little perspective from a Nigerian. Clearly, you have become a brother in arms in your work, in your education and so on, here in the United States with African Americans on African America, in people of color issues. I want to go back. Before you came to this country, what was your impression of African Americans in this country?

Dr. Amuwo: You know, I knew very little. I knew very little because I went to Methodist Boys High School for people who lived in Lagos at that time.

Alice: You went to what?

Dr. Amuwo: Methodist Boys High School.

Alice: Methodist. Okay.

Dr. Amuwo: It was only a male school. It was only meant for kids who were trying to go into science and going to do medicine. I was lucky.

David: Like an early STEM school.

Dr. Amuwo: Yes, it's similar to that. We were training so we can...we call it bio zoo botany, that's zoo botany, biology, zoology, botany that's what we were doing and physics of course. There were a lot of trade unionists in Nigeria at that time. You know, this is mid '60s. Nigeria had just gotten independence. We were just starting Biafra War. Communist Russia was trying to recruit smart kids to come to Russia so we can have perspective of Russia. We knew of the presence of Americans and we really admired [them]. In fact, there is no child when I was growing up who did not admire Black Americas.

David: Because of the struggle, or why was that?

Dr. Amuwo: We knew little of the struggle. That's the good thing. Our connection was through music.

David: Motown.

Dr. Amuwo: Yes.

David: Jazz.

Dr. Amuwo: Our connections were through ...not even jazz, you know. We knew about James Brown. James Brown actually came to Nigeria.

David: That's right, he sure did.

Dr. Amuwo: We knew about Cassius Clay at that time, so our connection, the idea was everybody wanted to be an American.

David: Now what of them, because I want to get into this a little bit. What was it about James Brown, Ali? Was it the energy in the face of all sorts of racism we all were experiencing? Their sense of overcoming? What was it? What was the essence of it?

Dr. Amuwo: We weren't educated to understand the slavery. We weren't educated to understand the movement at that time, but we were being educated to understand that we had some brothers and sisters somewhere who left from the shore and they seemed to excel in meaningful ways in terms of art and music. We didn't even know more so about contributions to science, you know what I'm saying? The everyday struggles of African Americans were somewhat oblivious to us. When I was growing up, we didn't know all about the struggle at all. In fact, what I knew is that if many of us knew the struggle and the behavior of [the] general white population to black people, many of us would probably not come here at all.

David: Fascinating.

Alice: Interesting.

Dr. Amuwo: They would probably not come here at all.

David: Because it would feel like what you had just come out of.

Dr. Amuwo: Yes, because what we were thinking was there it was a land of opportunity and everybody excels and you can work hard, do what you have to do, you have the opportunity to excel. That was what was being sold to us, but there were no people on the ground. The Russians, they did a great job in which you would go to high school. Every high school would have smart kids in a workshop. I remember [the] first Saturday of every month—every month usually represented by the unions—and the intention was to help us to come to Russia. We went to ... all those Soviet Union countries. They were recruiting us to do medicine. Of course the religious groups, Christian groups, they are recruiting also for people to come here. But for people who had relationship with Biafra war, I think there's quite a lot of campaigning going on. The Biafra had already portrayed Nigeria as being against Biafra. If you look even today you will notice that very little Hausa you will see.

David: Yes, very true. It's Yoruba, Ibo.

Dr. Amuwo: In the U.S.

Alice: Yes and let me ask you a question. Talk more about how you actually went to Russia to school for a while.

Dr. Amuwo: Let me tell you how I got there. I didn't go to Russia. This is what happened. I was to start school in Russia. They're admitting a year in advance; they're admitting now to come September or August of the following year. I was to start in August in 1970, since I go to the United States. My brother was already here.

Alice: In high school.

Dr. Amuwo: I was in high school, just finished high school and I was doing what we call HSC. It's called higher school certificate. It's meant for kids who want to go to university to do science like botany, biology.

David: Sort of an accelerated program on the science track. Is that fair?

Dr. Amuwo: Yes, to get [to] university.

David: To get to university.

Alice: Were you familiar with the Patrice Lumumba University in Moscow?

Dr. Amuwo: Yes.

Alice: Okay, I have been there. I just wanted to know.

Dr. Amuwo: Patrice Lumumba University was one of the premiere universities. You have to be extraordinarily smart, very, very smart and actually know people. Some of the children of union leaders actually ended up at Patrice Lumumba. A friend of mine that I actually went to see, he was here, I went to see him two weeks ago while I was in Nigeria. His name is Goodluck. That's his name Waha Goodluck. His father was the president of the trade union in Lagos at that time. He actually went to Patrice Lumumba University where he studied medicine.

David: Any relation to the current Goodluck?

Dr. Amuwo: No. No relationship at all. At that time they were smart. The Russians were smart. We had concentration of groups all over the place talking to kids: "Come to Russia. They will give you full scholarship." At the same time we had the church groups talking to kids; but more so, people learn for the most part because they were mostly responding to the crisis between Nigeria and Biafra, because they portray Biafra as sovereigns. The churches were helping Biafra; they were helping the Igbo to get here while the Russians were helping everybody else. I was one of those people admitted. There were really eight of us who were in the same community, in the same area that I was living in, in Lagos. It was everything paid for, scholarship, absolutely everything.

It was different from the other people that were coming here. From what we understood, they had to work. If you went to Russia, you didn't have to do anything. You didn't have to do anything. Everything is paid. I was to come in August, right? I was to go to Russia in August. Then again, my father really didn't want me to hang around, like the kids are hanging around who don't have anything to do in the summer.

Alice: In the spring time.

David: Too much idle time.

Dr. Amuwo: Yes. That man was just so worried. So my brother sent for me. I came here to live with my brother.

David: All right. Take a moment, take a sip.

Dr. Amuwo: That's really how I actually got here.

David: So you land. What are your impressions now? You have James Brown, you have some ideas sort of. Now what do you think?

Dr. Amuwo: My impression, remember now this was supposed to be the land…

David: It's supposed to be the land of opportunity. It's glowing when you land.

Golden streets, the whole bit, right?

Dr. Amuwo: Exactly. So my brother was living in 1745 E. 67th Street, 1645 I'm sorry.

David: Right over here. This is '72?

Dr. Amuwo: No, no this is '71.

David: Seventy-one. Okay, because the reason I asked, I want to put [it] in perspective.

Dr. Amuwo: I was actually supposed to start in the medical school in Russia, one of these Communist colleges, Stuttgart, in August of 1971.

David: Okay, yes.

Dr. Amuwo: My brother kind of screwed everything up so I ended up here. I came here January 1, 1971.

David: January 1, 1971. Paint a little picture for us. I would say listeners, normally, if we were on radio; but for the readership. So '71 Chicago, still dominated by the old man... Richard J. Daley. This community was just emerging and a few African Americans were beginning to show up here. There's not a lot of us here because we weren't here; hugely separated segregation in the city, certain streets you take your life in your hands if you cross going either west or too far south. If you go to Beverly you may never return. You go back to Western [Avenue] in those days you may never return. If you go downtown... we were not really invited to do that.

Dr. Amuwo: I didn't even know downtown.

David: You get a sense of it; but then I want to contrast that. So now you're here, it's January, cold as hell, right?

Dr. Amuwo: Very cold, very cold.

David: Talk to me about that moment.

Dr. Amuwo: January was in terms of the neighborhood I was in, this street here, that part was lined with a lot of homes, was lined with...

David: Very nice little businesses.

Dr. Amuwo: Yes and city fraud. There was quite a lot of crime in that area. We were told not to go to 67th and Stony Island. About the summer of 1971, I had walked to south of the big club. I was told that I couldn't cross the street, so I did; but I did not mostly to defy anyone, but because I didn't really remember I wasn't supposed to be there. So they tried to arrest me. They were playing golf.

They tried to arrest [me] for being there and asked me what was I looking for. I said, "I was just taking a walk." That was really my first instance in terms of, even I would see things on TV, in terms of what's really happening in terms of the discrimination. You know where you arrive and you stay among your people. You don't stay outside, so except when you see in TV, you don't really experience anything unless you kind of go out of your way. That was my first experience, but since that time…you kind of get used to the issue of black and white. These were issues that I never knew about when I was at home; and the issue of the land of milk and honey was put to rest.

David: Quickly, so much for that.

Dr. Amuwo: I had to work very hard. I got a job in this place called Choose Biscuit. The Choose Biscuit right here on 35th Street. I had to take a bus.

David: Yes, west on 35th.

Dr. Amuwo: I was mopping the floor. We didn't tell our parents at home that that's what we were doing.

Alice: Of course not.

Dr. Amuwo: My brother said, "You better not say anything."

Alice: That's right.

Dr. Amuwo: I didn't say anything. I entered UIC. I go from that to UIC. Then one day the guy came up to us, the foreman. We didn't know that he was also packed. I didn't realize at that time that one of the ways to actually keep your job [was] that we were supposed to give something back to the foreman. We got up, this Friday was pay day, and the guy says this is his money and I even went and followed. He fired all of us, except one person. We were fired from that one person. This guy—a good friend who just passed two months ago—he had to pay him. He was paying him.

David: The Chicago way.

Dr. Amuwo: Yes, he was paying him. So we were fired that day. I didn't know what to do. I had to pay tuition at UIC. It wasn't a lot of tuition, but I had to pay tuition. I got a bus when I was coming home on 35th Street. We were working overnight and that was about 10:00 o'clock in the morning. I was in the bus. I saw: Dishwasher for Hire. Oh boy. I got off the bus, went in there and he hired me. One thing about that time is that it was so easy to get a job.

David: You just walk in.

Dr. Amuwo: Yes, and you just knock on [the] door: "Are you hiring?" Yes, we're hiring. Come on in." There were vacancies all over the place. It was so easy to get a job. They hired me. I had never washed dishes in my life. I had never even seen a dishwasher machine. They guy hired me. So I was looking at this machine: What am I going to do with this? I said, "How do you do?" "I thought you said you were a dishwasher." "Yes I am." He told me how to do it. The guy saw that I was so slow doing it. That was at 10:00 o'clock. By 3:00 o'clock I was fired again. There was no telephone at that time; there was no telephone you can [use to] call home. I had to find a phone. Threw a dime in there. I think it was a dime or a nickel you had to put in there. I called my brother and say, "Are you home?" He said, "I'm home." "Well, they fired me." My brother just went crazy on me. "You are lazy. You're first person I've ever seen fired as a dishwasher." He said, "Well you said you wanted to go back home, so you need to go back home." I said, "I'm ready to go back home," because you have two way ticket, you've got TWA. I get home, I get to the apartment he said, "You're really going back home." "Yes, I'm going back." Because there was no phone to call home and my brother he was also struggling, but he said no you not going back. "What about the school?" I said, "I'm going back home. I still have my Russian scholarship, I'm going back." Somehow they convinced me and I didn't go back. I got another job, I went to UIC.

David: Let me ask. So it sounds like the community accepted you even though you were Nigerian and …you're now entrenched in the community for the most part. How were you accepted? How did you interact with the

African Americans?

Dr. Amuwo: Mostly interactions, they take place also because my brother was here. He had friends and most of the people that I know, I know they are from home and they had friends who were African Americans.

David: You were introduced into the community.

Dr. Amuwo: Yes, at that time it was easy to meet people. You know you're a kid of about twenty-three, twenty-four, twenty-five, and on Saturday we drag ourselves to their home...next Saturday we come to your home, you come to mine.... That's how I got to know them. I didn't really develop any real relationship with any white person. I didn't and I don't really know why. Maybe because I was so entrenched in my black community that I can't speak, except my boss when I was working for the university. I can't speak of any white person whose home I have ever been for dinner.

David: Even now.

Dr. Amuwo: Even now. People in higher office like the chancellor will invite you for dinner when you go to faculty or you get promotion or the president will invite you and you just have to be among other people.

I never really had any relationship with a white person, but [it] wasn't by design. Maybe anyone that they developed a relationship with me and I was never more so radical, but I feel many things to get me to understand that I'm really entrenched in the struggle of Black community, even though my experience was a little bit different so I never did.

I went to UIC I finished and ...I ended up doing the PhD. There were 5 percent black [students] in [the] master's degree [program] at that time and there were zero in PhD and I was to correct that. When they hired me I said this is what I wanted to do. I said my interest was to really get Black people to go to college. Nobody will hire you for a job; give you anything else because they know that you're not going to be successful.

David: Right, no directions, nothing, just a title.

Dr. Amuwo: It's a name. I met some people; they told me, "If you really want to be successful at this job you need to find money." I didn't know anything about finding money. Where do I find money? I have a job that pays me. Who cares? I went to meet with my boss at that time, his name [was] Luis Ruiz.

David: Luis.

Dr. Amuwo: Luis Ruiz, he was the associate dean. He said, "Well, I mean you're being paid. This is your job: you go out recruiting students." So I wrote a grant. It was about probably $105,000 for three years. I wasn't funded, so the following year, I wrote the grant again with some improvement. Ruiz called me and said to me, "You're getting it, ... you're going to be funded." It was through [the] federal government. It was a very competitive grant.

I thought I was already funded, but Ruiz told me that the school of public health was not ready for what I was trying to do, more so the focus on black people. They were expanding to focus on blacks and Hispanics. Ruiz told me that, "We aren't ready for this kind of stuff that you're doing. I said, "Well maybe I need to form a group starting from my basement. Maybe I can do something."

I was included as assistant dean for student and alumni affairs. My main thing was to bring students in. I studied the fact that one of the major problems is black people getting admitted [lacked] writing skills. They would write very poorly. Even though they [may] have done very well in their college, this was graduate school now. My grant was to look for avenues to give additional support to Africans. If you're coming in next year I start working with you from this year. I met Ruiz' wife. Nice woman. She was a professor at the Oakton College.

David: Oakton Community College.

Dr. Amuwo: I talked to his wife about it ... and [I] said, "You do things part time don't you?" She said "Yes." "You're hired! Can you work on this project for me?" That's how my program started.

Alice: Excellent.

Dr. Amuwo: Actually that program over years became the number one program in the country. I received more than 20 million dollars over time. I recruited the first Black ever to get a PhD at UIC [in] public health. What I really want to get to is that by the time I was retiring July 1, 2014, Congressman Luis Stokes, Danny K. Davis, all of them got together and invited me to the congress and they gave me a clock and inscribed my name.

David: Wow! Congratulations.

Dr. Amuwo: I inspired public health medicine and nursing. Danny [Davis] was the one that, you know Danny at UIC is in several professional districts and he knew of my struggle. He knew how I went from zero PhDs to about twenty-five PhDs.

David: Excellent.

Alice: In your travels, if you've had occasion, do you have any sense of how nowadays Black Americans are considered outside the United States?

Dr. Amuwo: Okay you know one of the challenges I've seen over time, you know I'm interested in this community that is very, very difficult to come across African Americans once you leave these shores of [the] U.S.

Alice: It's difficult to what?

Dr. Amuwo: It's very difficult to come across any African American maybe sometimes in the university sectors and sometimes because of the places I go, some people in business, might see me differently, but I meet my friends and my relatives who are married to African Americans. It's through them I meet African Americans.

           At one time it was so strong because there is a group called Naija wives. They are African American women married to Nigerian men. Many of them will live in Nigeria for a while and come here. Many of them are here now. Most of them are in their early sixties. They would have these annual parties, like [for] the 4th of July. It was always a big deal to them and they would invite us.

Alice: They're living outside the U.S.?

Dr. Amuwo: No, no they were living in Nigeria.

Dr. Amuwo: That's why they formed Naija wives, because they were living in

Nigeria, but over time they did not want to live in Nigeria, but drifting back here after some time, when their kids became of school age, they were drifting back little by little. Many are still there. The second area where I would meet would be at the university setting. When I became an assistant professor and I would want to meet my colleagues in Nigeria, in Lagos especially I will meet once in a while some African Americans or when I relate with some of my cousins who actually have collaborated in terms of business dealing, in terms of commercial related issues, I would meet up with Americans.

Alice: Were whites around in that time outside the country? Did they say anything ever about Black Americans?

Dr. Amuwo: One of the initial challenges is that you know, until recently it was very difficult to actually shake off the colonial influence in Nigeria and we went through all these military iterations, therefore they will, if not till now really it doesn't make sense except people don't want to admit it, if you and I went to Nigeria today, and you bring a white person with us, in due time that white person will take over everything and they will relate to him or her. If they are paying you like one million naira they probably pay us about one third of that.

David: What have you noticed has changed if anything? Well, you came and saw all the African American community and where it is now? What differences have you seen?

Dr. Amuwo: What has changed over time, a reduced sense of relationship, a reduced sense of community. It's really bad, very bad, very, very bad, because I had friends. I had more friends who were African American at that time than I had now. I see even my college mentors, but in terms of people that I have and the people that work for me, I'm surrounding my students and working on their dissertation, many of them are African Americans. Many of them are second generation Nigerians who were actually born here. I mean they are in their own entity. They have their own entity. They're different.

David: I follow what you mean. They're different.

Dr. Amuwo: My children one of them...

David: They don't connect. They don't seek to connect.

David: Here's the stunner, here is where I'm going to challenge you Dr. Amuwo. How do we change it back? How do we recreate the sense of community? What do you think needs to happen?

Dr. Amuwo: Well, you know I always hate to use whatever reason.

David: I'll say it so there needs to be some kind of revolution in some way.

Dr. Amuwo: We really need to think differently. We need to think differently in terms of it's no longer a matter of boycotting, but really to see that if something doesn't happen, this is what will happen. Is it possible that the whole of South Shore can just sit down at Lakeshore Drive and say that, "unless this happens, unless people can get money the violence including this community we won't let up." I'm telling you that we need change. We're not fighting now, right. We just sit on each other, the white folks will not need to get to work, the black, nobody will get to work.

Alice: That's very interesting.

Dr. Amuwo: We just sit down.

David: It's interesting, Doc, because...

Dr. Amuwo: Listen they are not going to kill us.

David: Among progressive people behind me Richard Mohammed, all these folks they're all kind of getting to the same place. We're getting there, but we need to trigger it.

Dr. Amuwo: The difference is that now we have white collar jobs. Now we are making some money.

David: Now we live in Lake Forest and you know.

Dr. Amuwo: Because we're never going to win, some of these folks...

David: They keep changing the rules.

Dr. Amuwo: They keep changing the rules unless we do something. This is what I see it's not going to happen, and if we build coalitions, coalition no longer helps us. I know the reason I know let's say we build a coalition of Hispanics and African Americans and this and that is not enough.

Number two...

David: If I may add, they've learnt to take the best of what we give and apply to them.

Dr. Amuwo: ...because I've spent the last thirty years bringing African Americans and Hispanics to public health, they worked for me, they were my students. I started thinking, really thinking the one I'm advocating for, minorities, African Americans and Hispanics, my Spanish brothers and sisters were just advocating for Hispanics.

David: Themselves.

Alice: Amen.

Dr. Amuwo: That is part of the individual problem and as soon as they excel they're going to see themselves as out of trouble.

David: No longer need the coalition.

Alice: I have to tell that's exactly what the Black students, only a handful of them did in the 19 early '70s in the Northwestern University, they sat down.

Dr. Amuwo: I remember you were the dean then.

Alice: This is before.

Dr. Amuwo: Before you became the dean.

Alice: That was what they won, they won the Black house. They were smart enough to demand institutional change and so now here we are what is it, 50 years later and we're fighting to keep the Black house because these youngsters have forgotten what that is for African Americans.

Dr. Amuwo: They have forgotten. They have forgotten the real value and they don't see it. I mean my kids they have PhD, they have MDs and they're still in the black community where their thinking is right. I would suggest this. "What do you think we should do?" "We should do things that will make home."

David: What's your...and I have to say I agree completely, in fact I talk about this all the time, but we see these little eruptions Black Lives Matter, the students at Mizzou what do you think of that?

Dr. Amuwo: It's not enough, those things will dwindle as time goes on because sometimes they know how to get us, so we have ten people in leadership positions. I get four of them, I give them good jobs in Wall Street and …that's the end of it. They know how to get us.

David: They know how to play both ways.

Dr. Amuwo: I'm not talking about individual achievement and individual progress.

David: A major strike.

Dr. Amuwo: A major strike, a peaceful strike to the extent that everybody will do it. Listen remember the Wall Street struggle.

David: Oh yes we sat in the room with the…

Dr. Amuwo: If there was a struggle, it could have been very successful beyond that. It was because it was high-jacked by some folks and while high-jacking it becomes more conservative in their thinking. We're talking about doing things together at the same time, the same day the same room and do it with a plan. You plan that one million people will sit in Lakeshore. To plan one million people will be on the bridge collecting dust, we're just sitting down, we're not doing anything. We're just sitting there, are you crazy? What do you want? This is what wants. It doesn't matter: we are never going to take over the congress. It's not going to happen.

David: No, never. It's fixed. All of that is fixed. It's owned by the power elite, so to try and operate in that paradigm will never work. It's doomed to fail.

Dr. Amuwo: Then what do we do? We'll just be trolling along little by little for the next century, unless we do something big that's impactful.

David: Absolutely agree.

Dr. Amuwo: It's very difficult to have the likes of Martin Luther King because people like that just come but once in a century; people that can really galvanize. We have people that galvanize people now, but it's not…

David: Not the same.

Dr. Amuwo: ...it's not enough, even Black Lives Matter and all those things, politics and the things they are doing you forget about it in a couple of years.

David: Doctor, do you have many closing... [comments]?

Dr. Amuwo: My closing remarks [are] the fact that we need to see us as one rather than us against them. I know. There are some black people here that are not really black, that are just high-jacking the opportunity, the Hispanics do it, everybody else do[es] it. Why do you need to separate? Because if we don't separate ourselves we have greater numbers.

David: And we can accomplish more.

Dr. Amuwo: We can accomplish more.

2. KENYA

Christopher K. Wambu

Christopher K. Wambu was born in a small village in Kenya. Since coming to the United States in the early seventies he has been a committed political and educational activist in Chicago and in New York. Wambu has taught economics and political science at Hunter College in New York for over three decades and continues to be a very popular instructor at the institution. In addition to teaching, Wambu has served for ten years as the international finance trustee at the historic Abyssinian Baptist church in Harlem, New York. Wambu regularly works with Rev. Dr. Calvin O. Butts III and Buzz Palmer to bring noted international speakers to address the congregation and the community. This is one example of his continued work combatting racism and xenophobia in the United States and abroad.

Wambu holds a bachelor's degree in political science from the University of Illinois at Chicago, a master's degree in political science from Ohio University and he has done extensive graduate study at Syracuse University in New York.

Without Advocacy from American Blacks, Freedom from Colonial Rule in Africa Would Have Taken Much Longer

My earliest contact with African Americans started early in my life, though not of physical nature. As I was growing up in rural Kenya during the early sixties, my frequent visits to the capital city of Nairobi began to include a visit to the United States Information Service Library. I visited there in search of something of value to read, driven by hunger for knowledge, and the need to expand and improve my limited knowledge of the world beyond my rural village in Kenya. Kenya at the time was a British colony, therefore for the Africans, that meant deprivation of any kind of knowledge or information, and limited to the typical colonial propaganda which was of very little use for the Africans. There were two public libraries with scanty choices, often limited to the glorification of the British Empire. At the time, understanding of Africa and Africans by Europeans was defined by serious misunderstanding, often full of willful and arrogant presumptions, excessive egotism, superiority and hubris on the part Europeans, and the literature they stocked in these two libraries reflected their social and political objectives in Africa. The USIS library was richer, and more diverse. More importantly, I once spied a magazine, titled *Ebony*. It had mainly what I believed were black looking people, though I was not quite sure. The women in the pictures looked very striking, which of course increased my curiosity. Needless to say that reading *Ebony* monthly left a mark, and perhaps a dream of someday visiting wherever these people were located.

My next encounter was in the Democratic Republic of the Congo. There, in 1967, I met a young lawyer from New York City, named Robert Van Lierop. He was on a culture tour organized by NAACP. We met in the airport bus. We began to converse, perhaps isolated by our grave circumstances, for we could not speak French or Lingala, but we both spoke English. He identified himself as Afro-American meaning Black, but the claim at the time for me was not compelling, given his complexion. He understood my suspicion, as well as confusion, and carefully began to narrate the complexities of racial classifications in United States. He explained that Blacks were not monolithic in pigmentation, and that the binary classification of races in the United States was a racist ploy to divide people and propagate racism. I learned much from him, and we became brothers, and have remained to this day.

My next encounter with African Americans was in Chicago, where I had settled to go to college. While I resided in the north side, I became a frequent participant in political and social activities on the south side of Chicago. I was also a very active political activist within the African American community, alongside an African American activist named Prexy Nesbit and his late sister. From them I learned a lot about the African American community, in Chicago and beyond.

Perhaps the best encounter was when I met my late wife Judith Martin Wambu in 1972. She was my Swahili student, albeit not a good one, and I equally her student in an English class at University of Illinois at Chicago. In the end we decided to raise the ante and got married. Most of my social and political encounters with African Americans have remained intact and have enriched my stay in the United States, way beyond what I could have imagined or dreamed in the 1960s. They have exposed me to a world that I never knew existed, enriched me, and made me politically whole. I should say—before coming to America—I had met informally with interesting African Americans in Nairobi, Kenya. I met or rather saw Dr. James Herman Robinson, the founder of Operation Crossroads Africa, when they came to build a health clinic in my region; and coincidentally forty years later, I was to attend a church service at Church of the Master of Morning Heights in Manhattan of which he was the founder, a few blocks from my current home.

I went to listen to Louis Armstrong during his African tour in early sixties, which was part goodwill ambassadorship presumably organized by United States Information Services. I saw Ralph Bunche when he briefly stopped at a school named after him in Nairobi. While such encounters sound insignificant and trivial, for us Africans living in a British colony they were important, opening windows to a world we did not know existed. Whether Ralph Bunche and Louis Armstrong were progressives or not, the British government—which had a monopoly of power—had made sure that contact between blacks in the United States and Africa could only develop with the complacent cooperation with the American government, meaning in their own terms and interests. So for us, meeting these African Americans at the time was crucial in widening our social and political horizons because before, who we met was often dictated by the American and British governments, depending on their political imperatives. But we did not know that then.

African Americans, despite their status as underdogs in the United States on all social indexes, continue to be the iconic, cultural beacons of the United States to the world. They continue to be the microscopes under which America's cultural components are scrutinized and assessed. Their inclusion in the American cultural mosaic makes American culture palatable even for those who suffer from the "Ugly American Syndrome". They have added a positive image to United States abroad, and diluted the negative aspect of America's cultural, diplomatic misdeeds by giving the United States a very human face, and positive evaluation—even when America barely deserves it. Are African Americans accepted abroad? Overall, very much so. We must remember that America's approach to race, "the binary approach", the idea that there are only two races that matter—one more superior than the other—is not a conventional one, nor does it have social utility outside the United States.

It is a peculiar trend confined to America. Nor is race an important social index in assessing individuals' social merit. Once you exist in the United States, the classification over who you are changes, and so does the value judgement index that comes with it. This does not mean that African Americans are not black in Paris, Bombay, Nairobi or Cairo. It just means that being black no longer carries negative social connotations. It is a change that confuses even African Americans, who by and large have internalized racial parameters in the United States and are often at a loss once designated or confronted with the common global citizenship.

It is these experiences that have led many African American political observers to question and challenge the premise on the tenets of the creed in the Declaration of Independence, the Preamble of the Constitution, and the Bill of Rights, concluding that America could have become a meritocratic nation, and that Dr. King's dream of being judged according to individual merit rather than color would have borne fruit had America actually believed in the merit of the American creed. Instead they continue to subscribe to Gunnar Myrdal's conclusions, that incorrectly attribute racist beliefs to prejudices, antipathies and selfishness of various white groups and individuals; but somehow that prejudice and racism are irrational and aberrant responses in a society whose core value system is the American creed.[1]

In my opinion, the most important period in African American history can be traced to that period in time when African Americans in the former Confederate states lost that psychological fear of the white system, white supremacists, and decided to disobey, disregard all racist, immoral laws, racist traditions and norms that had governed their lives before and after the Civil War. These laws, norms and traditions had oppressed them, exploited them, and denied them their natural rights and privileges of citizenship. When Rosa Parks said "No, I won't be moved," that defiance became a milestone in the history of African Americans. It demonstrated that the "emperor had no clothes." Though it did not end the struggle or racism, it gave the struggle a new calculus, one that white racists could not have predicted.

Blacks were no longer afraid. You could shoot them, bring the dogs, water cannons, batons; but blacks were no longer prisoners of fear. That was a historical, political U-turn, one that brought universal freedom closer in America and the world. It is to be noted that this political event helped to transform the whole world. People, nations who had imagined freedom as a pipe dream began to visualize it in their own life experiences. It encouraged people to rise up and demand not just freedom, but equality and recognition of their humanity. For that reason, I would award African Americans the highest tribute in furthering universal freedom for the whole world, in challenging a big power like the United States—which took courage—and winning. They encouraged others to dream, to hope and to fight back.[2]

There are many African Americans who, in my view, influenced me and others, by the way they lived and their contribution to the world. I would highlight individuals like Paul Robeson or his selflessness, the willingness to sacrifice self-interest so that his fellow men—black or white—can realize their individual dreams. Robeson could have made it in Hollywood and made a lot of money, but instead chose to share his endowments with the rest of us. I have great respect for Adam Clayton Powell, who was a congressman and senior pastor of Abyssinian Baptist Church. Powell used his seniority in Congress to advance the rights of the lower classes in education and labor. His legislation in education has enabled many working class children to go to college; and I have never failed to remind my students at Hunter College that without Powell's advocacy and courage to fight economic injustice, they would not be in college today.

I also have high regard for Dr. Calvin O. Butts, the senior pastor at Abyssinian Baptist Church in New York City for his willingness to put up a struggle in uplifting the poor in New York City and beyond. His leadership in the church has led in increasing affordable housing in New York City, quality education, and other important social services, including housing for senior citizens. I have been honored to serve as trustee at Abyssinian and I bear witness to extensive work of this church in New York City and Africa as well.

I must say having met and befriended Buzz Palmer and his wife Dr. Alice Palmer has given me a resource, a foundation, a sense of commitment to change, that otherwise is not always common to African immigrants. Buzz and Alice have included me, invited me to some of the most important, active political forums around the world. For that, I owe them a lot. I must say without reservation that my late wife Dr. Judith Martin Wambu was equally instrumental in my political education as well as social integration into the African American community. Though I joined and familiarized myself with my social and political network in the 1970s, we made sure that our children were socialized in a progressive environment, including starting college at traditional Black colleges. We made sure that their social interaction was dominated by people who shared our social and political values. We made great efforts to expose them to the African and African American world, without depriving them of the world view. All these children's growth and maturity has been progressive, remarkable, and rewarding: Muthoni in D.C. involved in political works; Kamau Mcbee in Baltimore in environmental biology; Zella Palmer in New Orleans as chair of Ray Charles Culture Institute; Wanja Wambu with IMF an architect; and many other young people who have developed under the auspices of this common community alliance.

My views on African Americans may not reflect that of the general society in Kenya. My views are shaped by my personal experiences, exposures and direct participation, including my assimilation and integration within the African American community on issues both social and political. This is true in all the places I have lived, especially Chicago and New York City. Kenyans' general views and attitudes towards African Americans is usually through the media, often imported television programs, and occasional physical encounter.

As explained elsewhere in this essay, these distortions—good and bad—are often molded by the stereotypes that continue to prowl in the mainstream media. There is, of course, a bias in favor of sports figures and people in the entertainment industry. Of course, the era of Obama, a descendant of a Kenyan father, has added its own political dosage to the drama. How much of this Obama mania improved the African American image in Kenya and Africa is difficult to gauge. Obama himself has not entertained this form of political narrative, preferring instead on highlighting his role as the president of the United States, and its relationship with the world, of which Africa plays only an insignificant role. It is to be noted that Obama did not visit Kenya until nearly the end of his term in office. In addition, he has kept Kenyan's leadership at arm's length, preferring to follow Washington's traditional modus operandi—i.e., check with former colonial powers first, instead of direct contact with Africans— and like his predecessors, rarely does the Obama administration contradict Western Europe on Africa. Nor have they shown initiative or inclination to develop a direct, new and constructive linkage with Africa; hence America's loss in competitive edge to China, especially in trade and diplomacy.

> **"We must learn that passively to accept an unjust system is to cooperate with that system, and thereby to become a participant in its evil."**
> Martin Luther King, Jr.

On Black American leaders, most Africans know about Martin Luther King, Malcolm X. On contemporary black leaders, many Africans are familiar with individuals like Jesse Jackson, Andrew Young. African governments have developed political sophistication and know how to lobby the Congressional Black Caucus.

In reference to my countrymen, I think most of their views on African Americans now are shaped by TV: The Bill Cosby Show, Oprah and other entertainment soap operas. It is a view that creates distortions, both negative and positive. It also sustains stereotypes, especially with rap music and the music videos. It lacks intellectual component a disadvantage to those less educated. The mainstream American media has also added its poisonous dosage on the image of the African American social portfolio. It does in Africa what it does here—that is, circulates a negative gospel, one that highlights the negatives; black on black crime, slums, street life, underclassness, all without explaining the root cause of these social dynamics as they exist; the historical origins, how they are sustained and who benefits.

More devastating to the African American image is the absence of any positive images on the community, their contributions towards Americanisms. Africans rarely get to learn about African Americans who are contributing positively to the United States and the world, as doctors, lawyers, teachers, businesspeople, etc. They rarely get to learn that African Americans have been the vanguard of America's industry revolution and every other industrial and cultural development in America. Recently, a good friend of mind in Kenya asked me if my late wife was "a negro". I admitted that she was, among other identities, and academic titles. Does that mean African Americans are regarded with disdain, indifference, or admiration? I would say admiration; but sometimes for the wrong reasons, often misguided.

The African American community includes Michael Jordan, Mike Tyson, Bill Cosby. But these are not the pillars of the community, however great and famous their individual contributions may be. The African American community is not a monolithic group. There is diversity of individuals, who continue to help shape the world, make the world a better place, and demonstrate moral courage in opposing America's hegemonic tendencies.

Black colleges have made enormous contributions in educating the first layer of pre-independence African leaders. Among these are luminaries like the first president of Nigeria, Dr. Nnamdi Azikiwe, who attended Howard University and was taught by Dr. Ralph Bunche (Azikiwe later attended Lincoln University in 1930s). Dr. Kamuzu Bunda, who is the first president of Malawi, received a medical degree from Meharry Medical College in Tennessee in 1937. Dr. Kwame Nkrumah attended Lincoln University in 1939. There are many other distinguished Africans who went on to contribute enormously towards African political and economic changes as a result of the support and generosity from these traditional black colleges. [3]

Even when African students attended the all-white colleges, and many did, their social existence was sustained by the presence of African American communities in most of the major American cities. It is difficult to imagine life for these African students without the social support and comfort that African Americans provided, the social climate, the security. For many African students who settled in outlying all-white communities, the isolation had immediate effect, even without having to confront direct racism. Today, as a result of this pioneering bridge building, there are many more African immigrants who have settled comfortably in the United States. But the byproduct goes further and has all benefitted African immigrants in America immeasurably.

African immigrants to the United States are among the most educated groups in this country. Some 48.9 percent of all African immigrants hold college diplomas. This is more than double the rate of native-born white Americans and nearly four times the rate of native born African Americans. Immigrants from Africa typically settle in heavily urban areas upon arrival. There is a positive correlation between where Africans settle and the presence of African American communities, suggesting that the African Americans presence is a pull-factor, determining where Africans feel comfortable to make a home. [4]

Perhaps, with the exception of recent immigrants from Somalia and Southern Sudan—whose immigration circumstances are very different and their settlement dictated by the U.S. government— rarely do African immigrants settle too far from African American communities. Nor should it surprise us the speed at which these immigrants get transformed and integrated into the general African American community. Their lives, their day to day experiences, begin to mimic those of African Americans, and finally their children become integrated into the African American general population.

The image of the African American has changed over time. While the quality of those images could be debated, Africans know more about African Americans now than any other time. Technology has removed the information barriers. The Internet, TV, and social media have all collaborated in this endeavor. There is more exchange of information, frequent social contact, direct communications, etc.

Unfortunately, most of those contacts are not screened and come with a lack of any educational or cultural input. Without first filtering stereotypes and distortions, they tend to recreate negative images of both of the communities. What we need to do is remove stereotypes without distorting the truth and encourage the study of history without nationalistic jingoism and symbolic political bravados. This means avoiding the sentiments of fantastic achievements, unless it can be proved, and admitting that in Africa, as well as the United States, in black communities the struggle is ongoing—from the eighteenth to the twenty-first century. Then we can finally admit that—despite our best efforts—we have not reached the Promised Land.

To their credit, African Americans have been on the forefront in the liberation struggle of the African continent as well as other oppressed territories in Asia and South America.

Pan-African consciousness was molded by African Americans, including West Indians, before it found its way to the African continent. Writers and political activists such as Langston Hughes, Richard Wright, Du Bois, Marcus Garvey, George Padmore and many other like-minded individuals were instrumental in awakening the African continent, and igniting its potentiality. They advocated for decolonization, the end of the apartheid regime in South Africa, abolition of semi-slave regimes and full independence for all. Paul Robeson and George Padmore were the first to organize the first Pan-African Conference. In 1945, Pan-African conference was held in Manchester with DuBois, George Padmore, Appiah of Ghana, Kwame Nkrumah of Ghana (Gold Coast then), Jomo Kenyatta of Kenya, which became a pace-maker for decolonization in Africa and the British West Indies. Their demands included an end to colonial rule, abolishment of racial discrimination, and an end to imperialism around the world.[5]

It took an African American journalist named George Washington Williams to highlight and expose King Leopold's cruelty, rapaciousness and total lack of humane regard to the rubber tappers of the Congo. Leopold demanded more rubber, more of everything, and when Congolese workers failed to satisfy his greed, he amputated their arms. The exposure by Williams led to an international scandal, which in turn led to Leopold's loss of the Congo as a personal freedom. It is difficult to assess how much of this provided a relief for the Congolese, since the Congo remained a Belgium colony until 1960s. Williams' willingness to take the risk remains a commendable act.[6]

In comparison, despite Woodrow Wilson's anti-colonial declarations during the founding of the League of Nations, American mainstream politics had only modest anti-colonial credentials. Even at home, Woodrow Wilson himself could hardly be accused of excessive racial sensibility or even sympathy for the oppressed non-whites. African Americans, on the other hand, attended to the universal values, instead of the narrow Euro-centric oriented world view, or worse nationalistic interests.

For the most part, African Americans were alone in the United States in calling for a common human value, demanding those "inalienable rights" for all, which transcended race ethnicity, geography or nationalistic interest. Adam Clayton

Powell, the late Harlem congressman, senior pastor at Abyssinian Baptist Church, represented African Americans' viewpoint on the world during the Afro-Asian Solidarity Conference in Bandung, Indonesia in 1954. Thurgood Marshall was the senior constitutional advisor during Kenya's independence negotiation with Britain in 1960s, and was instrumental in the formulation and drafting of Kenya's first independence constitution. Even much earlier, African Americans were instrumental in spreading plantation farming to former German colonies in West Africa, and spreading Christianity in South Africa—for better or for worse in the nineteenth century. [7]

Paul Robeson and the other Pan-Africanists provided unreserved support to Ethiopia after it was invaded by the Italian dictator Benito Mussolini during the Second World War. It is no exaggeration to say that without African American political support, political independence to African colonies would have come, but it would have taken much longer, and at greater suffering. Apartheid would have collapsed; but, again, it would have taken decades more. [8]

African American relationships and association with people outside the United States has a special place in the history of man's struggle against political, economic, and cultural marginalization. Even more special is an established track record of the African American struggle for universal freedom. While other Americans— including the founding fathers—found serious economic obstacles in establishing universal freedom, African Americans embraced and propagated the very English and principally French philosophy on social contact, and the natural rights for all men, including the idea that labor was an individual private property and that no one can exploit an individual's labor without doing them great harm. Had the founding fathers subscribed to these principles, there would have been no slavery, no racism, no wealth inequality rooted in racism.

African American struggle has been the beacon for all struggling people around the world. While Martin Luther King might have incorporated the nonviolence strategy from Mahatma Ghandi, the struggle by African Americans resonated well with people across the globe, whether Christians, Muslims, Hindus, Black or White. Their struggle was in a global political language: people all over the world spoke the language, and it was understood across the globe. Though based in the United States, especially the South, it was not colored, or monopolized by local peculiarities; rather it had a global reach, and it awakened millions of oppressed, empowered and educated them, and gave them the engine to power the necessary social change.

While the rest of America engaged in self-congratulatory hype called "exceptionalism", African Americans saw themselves as global citizens, with a common interest with all those struggling to make the world a better place. They did not have to be persuaded to join the war against fascism. They needed no encouragement to crusade against colonialism, racism, and apartheid; or to support equality for women and the Native Americans.

But these interactions with others abroad have also added a dosage of broader world view. In return it has earned African Americans some level of respect, one that is often denied to the rest of America. Many African Americans have found cultural refuge in Europe and across the globe—from writers like James Baldwin and Richard Wright to jazz musicians and cabaret singers like Josephine Baker. In fact, we could say without exaggeration or contradiction that most of America's cultural attributes admired abroad has been exclusively African American.

So where do African Americans stand, at a time when the United States is being accused of hegemonic tendencies, economic and political chauvinism? Let us make one thing clear, African Americans are not outsiders looking in on America. They have been part of what we call "Americanness". Without the African American component, America has no story. They have been here since the founding of the country. They have built its economy, its infrastructures; they have been the vanguard of industry revolution. The feeling of pessimism, the feeling that African Americans are losing ground, becoming marginalized may have currency, but we have to study history.

American history and experience is full of the "rise and fall" of African Americans, nationally or regionally. In fact, African Americans' struggle is full of these cynical stories with ups and downs. This is their experience in America. I do not see a point in which African Americans will become irrelevant in the United States. If that happens, so many others will go down as well. What I think we need to do is think of African Americans in the twenty-first century, as industries outsource jobs outside the United States. What are young black people going to be doing? We need to think about education.

So many black youths are being written off the job market because they lack skills for contemporary industrial jobs. Those jobs are going to India and China. Should we revamp education to prepare these young people for future job markets? I think this is the new struggle. Let us not be caught unprepared. Let us not be surprised, as indeed we were with the 1877 great compromise.

Black people need to maximize their purchasing power in the United States and the world. I have heard people like Jesse Jackson highlight African American aggregate consumption level measured in dollars, which is perhaps close to Canada's GNP. The best figure to measure African Americans' power and influence in the economy would be in the production index. African Americans need to get involved in ownership of industries, wholesale and retail establishments, and in that way, the consumption GNP per capita could be sustainable to a point. They also need to get involved in the financial market, because only then can they assist black merchants to acquire credit lines, as well as financial advice.

All the same, African Americans can still redirect their disposable incomes in a direction that creates economic growth in their communities. Going to shop in a faraway shopping mall in Chicago suburbs impoverishes the west and south sides of Chicago. Investing your dollars in people and communities who do not do the same for you is nothing short of outsourcing wealth, for no return. Blacks have to start creating jobs in their communities, recycling the dollars in those communities. Only then could you generate economic growth in the south or west side.

On the diplomatic form, African Americans need to continue to raise their voices against policies that destroy the global community. It is patriotic to challenge policies that make your country look bad. African Americans need to challenge America when she tries to use her power to impose hegemonic political and unreasonable economic doctrines on countries that can ill afford them. African Americans need to raise their voices in support of progressive government, and institutions that promote human rights, and economic self-sufficiency. Perhaps, out of fear of offending and violating African pride, African Americans have often avoided critical evaluation of African dictators: Idi Amin in Uganda, Mobuto Sese Seko in DRC (Democratic Republic of the Congo), Moi in Kenya and the list goes on. Perhaps it is the fear of reinforcing traditional stereotypes of blacks, but this silence has not helped to eliminate the stereotypes anyway. On the other hand, these dictators are often on a murderous range, destroying the chances for these countries to develop, eradicate poverty, and illiteracy. Even xenophobic tendencies and behaviors in post-apartheid South Africa rarely get the attention they deserve. Those who fought against apartheid need to raise their voices with equal concern, perhaps even louder, against xenophobia among South African blacks against immigrant blacks from Mozambique, Zimbabwe, and Somalia. African Americans need to condemn terrorism imposed in Kenya, Nigeria and other areas of the world.

It is very important that African Americans stand up against dictatorship, tyranny expedience, as well as corruption in Africa. Like Martin Luther King before, who challenged the American governments to import or inject morals in politics, African Americans should do no less for Africa. They should insist on that moral component in governing in places like Kenya, Angola, Nigeria, South Africa, etc., where glaring wealth, matched by unbelievable inequality and conspicuous consumption by the rich remains a shameful badge of misrule. This despite rapid economic growth in these states. In these states, the economies continue to do well, while the majority of their populations continue to experience declining standards of living. Even more worrisome are regimes in Burundi, CAR (Central African Republic), Eritrea, Democratic Republic of the Congo, Equatorial Guinea, and Congo Brazzaville, with nefarious rulers, diabolical governments and appalling social-economic conditions.

We should be able to count on African Americans to keep the torch of freedom and liberation shining, and keep these dictators awake day and night. They should challenge the past American trends which were to support and sustain evil regimes, most of these led by an unscrupulous criminal without pangs of conscience, lacking moral caveats.

Footnotes:

1) Benjamin B. Ringer and Elinor R. Lawless, *Race Ethnicity and Society* (New York: Routledge Chapman Hall, Inc., 1989), 69.

2) Emmanuel Gerard and Bruce Kuklick, *Death in the Congo: Murdering Patrice Lumumba* (Cambridge: Harvard University Press, 2015), 56.

3) List of Lincoln University (Pennsylvania) Alumni: https://en.wikipedia.org/wiki/list of Lincoln University -- (Pennsylvania) – alumni: May 28, 2016

4) "Blacks in Higher Education," *The Journal of Education* 26 (Winter 1999–2000): 60–61.

5) The Pan-African Congress 1900-1965; The Black Past: Remembered and Reclaimed: HTTP://www.blackpost.org/perspectives/pan-african-congresses -- 1900-1945

6) Williams George Washington Report upon the Congo Free State: In Adam Hochschild: King Leopold's Ghost: The story of Greed, Terror and Heroism in Colonial Africa (Boston: Houghton Mifflin Company, 1999), 101–114. George Washington Williams: from Wikipedia, the free encyclopedia. https://en.wikipedia. org/wiki/George_Wahington_Williams

7) Henry F. Jackson, *From the Congo to Soweto: US Foreign Policy Towards Africa Since 1960* (New York: William Morrow and Company, 1982), 130–135.

3. SENEGAL

Doudou Diène

Doudou Diène, born 1941, was United Nations special reporter on contemporary forms of racism, racial discrimination, xenophobia and related intolerance from 2002 to 2008. Diène holds a law degree from the University of Caen (Normandy, France), a doctorate in public law from the University of Paris, a diploma in political science from the Institut d'Études Politiques in Paris, and an honorary doctorate degree in law from the University of the West Indies (Cave Hill, Barbados).

Earlier in his career, between 1972 and 1977, he served as Senegal's deputy representative to UNESCO. In 2011, he was appointed independent expert on the situation of human rights in Côte d'Ivoire.

Editor's Note: Occurrences in Doudou Diène's responses of the term "UN Decade of Afro-descendants" are references to the United Nations' initiative, the International Decade for People of African Descent.

Interview by David Robinson by phone
Grasping the Depths of Racism in America Changed Me

David: Well let's officially begin then, if you wouldn't mind, stating your name and your occupation?

Doudou: My name is Doudou Diène. I am a former UN special reporter on racism and the former director of UNESCO Division of Intercultural Dialogue. I was a director of the Slave Route Program which I launched in 1994. I am presently chair of International Coalition of Sites of Conscience.

David: Excellent, excellent thank you. Now we'll dive right in to the questions. What first bought you in contact with Black Americans and can you describe or give personal stories about how that happened and what your immediate observations were?

Doudou: You know, as an African I was evidently very much interested. I shouldn't be interested by the situation of Afro-descendants in the Americas. It means that since my childhood I was very much involved in documenting the situation of Afro-descendants and trying to understand to know to get contacts and slowly from my readings, from the movies from many things I start to be in touch. But the decisive moment was when I was in Paris, where I went to study. I met some Afro-American brothers and sisters throughout our scholars walk in Paris and also from the music, jazz and etcetera.

David: Excellent.

Doudou: The most important moment was when I was in UNESCO as director of the Division of Intercultural Dialogue. I launched in 1994 the UNESCO Slave Route Program. But before, David, I found out an important moment. I was appointed from '77 to '86 as director of the UNESCO office in New York at the UN. I was there for ten years almost and evidently it was a golden opportunity to get closer with Afro-descendants in the Americas.

David: Excellent, excellent and in the course of those early years, was there anything that surprised you or changed your thinking? Did you come into it with any preconceived notions that were changed? Or had you done enough study and seen enough of sort of their cultural influences so your thinking was confirmed? Was there anything that changed?

Doudou: The most important lesson I learn and the discovered almost is before getting to the U.S., I had a card of theoretical knowledge of the situation of enslavement and racism in the Americas. Yes, I knew racism in Europe and in France and in Africa, but it is when I was in the U.S. during those ten years as head of UNESCO in New York, and when I was engaged in defending UNESCO from the Americas during the Reagan years when the U.S. was planning to leave UNESCO and the UNESCO was attacked as being a kind of South World oriented and a terrorist organization by the Reagan administration.

When I started to fight back as head of UNESCO in New York, I was really in the eyes of the terrible human storm that I start moving around getting a first-hand look to the situation in the U.S. It was when I really started grasping the depth of what enslavement was, what racism was and is still. This was, I think, for me [a] very profound change.

David: Excellent, excellent. Digging a bit further in this question what would you say is the level of interest in the African American experience of those living outside the U.S., so some of your colleagues that were from other countries from other cultures? What would you say their thinking was?

Doudou: First I think it's important to state, to express one thing I am convinced of, because I learnt from my years in the U.S. and when I launched the Slave Route Program and during ten years I was head of this program, is that the fact in the African continent really don't know what slavery was. They certainly yes, they lost a parent, family members, relatives and all our oral tradition is full of stories of capture, of violence.

The depth of what enslavement was and racism was, Africans don't grasp it. It's a kind of theoretical experience, but it is really when I go to the U.S. and I saw the economic, social, political and cultural expression and the consequences of racism, that my view was absolutely profoundly and dramatically changed. Because this is where I start to understand that it is something which is very profoundly in the DNA of the history and culture of the Americans—not only the U.S., but all the sub-Americans and Caribbean.

David: Yes.

Doudou: No doubt that, David, when I was nominated as special reporter on racism from 2002 to 2008, we investigated it worldwide and one of my investigations was as you know in the U.S. I think in 2007 or [2008] which is where really I dig deeply because I went around. I came to Chicago also and certainly Beth and Alice were very helpful for me. I really realize that there is something there which we did not understand from outside. That we have to learn more and it will be a long way to uproot the legacy of slavery and racism.

David: Excellent, excellent and let's explore that a bit more. As you know, now there is a long history of defiance and struggle against all of the issues surrounding slavery and surrounding oppression. The African American community has spent the last four hundred plus years fighting against this terrible thing. It sounds like perhaps you hadn't heard yet of the resistance on the part of what was happening in our culture here in the United States and African Americans' constant struggle. Did you learn more about that and if so can you give any examples of moments or periods of resistance that moved you or helped you understand more about the situation?

Doudou: Good point David. First, I have been slowly grasping the depth of racism in the U.S. and during my years there as director of UNESCO in New York. It was deeper during my investigation when I stayed in the U.S. as UN special reporter. Two points I would like to give you as a reflection. One as I said I repeat that racism is something which is part of American culture and history DNA. It is very deeply rooted. Secondly, I do think that there has been progress, slow progress and the progress is firstly due to the permanent resistance not only of [the] enslaved, because the enslaved Afro-descendants keep fighting from the first day of capture to the transportation in the Atlantic, in the Middle Passage, the ships to the working conditions in the plantations in America.

They kept fighting and they kept fighting on two important fronts, not only they kept fighting physically, fighting physically with their body, but for me the most important struggle…is what I call the cultural resistance. What I call the main culture because the Afro-descendants and the enslaved Africans start in the context where they were considered not as human being because racism was an ideological pillar of Atlantic slave trade. They realized that their masters they did not see them as human. It is when the enslaved started to rely very deeply on their meat and their religion, on their culture, on the origin and all things which their master could not see because he considered them as not civilized.

They started to elaborate a very sophisticated process of resistance which is expressed on every aspect of their daily life. I give you a few examples. One what I call the spiritual resistance, because the masters tried to make the enslaved Christian because at that time the policy was that of the system and did not combat or condemn racism, but asked the enslaved to obey their master as the Christian bible.

When the enslaved were asked to become Christian and to worship the Christ and the Virgin Mary they could not say no, but what they did and it is one of the most profound expressions and refined expression of good resistance is to transform the figures of Virgin Mary and the Christ to African gods and orisha. They gave them in their heart, the hidden teachings and started worshipping them. They did it not only because they could not refuse, because they come from the spiritual tradition in Africa where everything is holy and all things are expression of God. The masters did not see this and this is why they very much used the expression of Christian worship by music, by whatever to return it, to transform it in expression of resistance.

Secondly, I give you another example. When the masters, people don't realize that the reason why festivals and carnivals are so popular in all the Western hemisphere and in the United States and the Caribbean, the origin of it David is that the slaves did ask the masters to organize regularly some kind of entertainment so that to enjoy them with their wife etcetera at certain moment. Certainly, the masters say, "Yes you can at one moment come and dance and do some things." What the slave did know was that the moment of festival and carnival was a moment where first they got together, because they were separated during all the years.

Secondly, they transform their suffering into an expression of artistic expression and culture and really hide it behind this cultural expression to display it in front of the master who did not see that meaning. Thirdly, it was a moment also for them to keep from this artistic expression the memory of their suffering and their life. What I'm saying is that you have another subtle and profound expression of cultural resistance.

I give you a last one. I come back to the spiritual tradition. When the masters ask them to worship the Christ and Virgin Mary, you know what they did in Brazil and Cuba? They integrated, as I said, the Virgin Mary and Christ in their African spiritual figures and they created Candomblé in Brazil and Santeria in Cuba. Well, side by side with African orisha, you can see the figures of the Christ of the Virgin Mary and now Candomblé is one of the spiritual pillars of Brazil and Santeria in Cuba.

Lastly, now what is highly important is the ethical resistance because it is where the women have played [a] very fundamental role. People don't realize that they were the pillars of the first of resistance because in the evening not only [did] the women participate to the physical resistance with her body and lost their life and suffered, but the women were the mothers and sisters. In the evening when the enslaved came back to their homes, the women were the persons to put them together and try to revive and regenerate their forces and give them more forces to keep going. This is where the figure of the woman has been the figure of regeneration of first physical and [then] the spiritual force.

What I'm saying, David, is that all this dimension has not been enough study because it is, in my view, the documentation of this cultural resistance is the only way to show that it is through control and spiritual resistance that the enslaved Africans regain, reconquer their humanity which was denied to them by the ideology of racism of the masters. It is to show that it is by using their culture and traditions that really throughout the centuries because it lasted centuries that not only they record the racism system, but at the end they won.

They won because they show that it is the humanity and spirituality which is beyond their body because limiting the resistance to the body, to the physical resistance is accepting the construction of racism which give to the enslaved the only advantage and possible victory against this human force its capacity as a work force. The enslaved demonstrated that they were beyond that. I think that this dimension has been going throughout African American histories. I do think that all the expression of blues, of jazz, of whatever the exclusion of art, the very profound vibration of gospels, all these show the depth.

I must say that one last expression is the struggle to establish the national museum of African history and culture in Washington. As you know, it took years of combat against the [U.S.] Congress...and instrumentally the Congress did vote it and now the museum is being built. What I'm saying is that the cultural and spiritual resistance has been a pillar of the enslaved combat and re-humanization and will continue being a pillar because, the last point, David, what makes racism so complex to combat is that it is very subtle. Its deeper expressions are in culture and spirituality, mostly in culture.

In cultural expression, language, art...they are very much hidden. The field of culture, art and the tradition are highly important in the long term to uproot racism, because you have to uproot racism not only socially, economically and politically, but to uproot it in the mindset in the way the cultural glasses are attempted in the Americas and the Caribbean. It will take a long time to wipe this cultural glasses.

David: This is a fascinating line of thinking. I am grateful that you raised it. In fact, you've answered four or five of my questions just in your response already, but I want to explore this cultural dynamism a bit further and ask you, in your travels and in your study have you seen the impact of African American culture? I think you're absolutely right. It comes out of resistance and in expression, spiritual expression. Have you seen this have impact beyond the United States and in other cultures? Of course, you know, we know that if you go to [the] far reaches of China, they know who Michael Jordan is and they know who Michael Jackson is and so on. Do you find this to be true in your travels that the expressions, spiritual and cultural expressions of the African American Diaspora are having impact worldwide?

Doudou: David, very much. Let me take three dimensions historically. We'll come back to the last point you make. Because, as you know, in my role [at] UNESCO I was in charge of launching the Silk Road Program, which was a program launched by UNESCO to study the cultural and human interaction between [the] so called East and West of the world. As you know, I organized international expeditions in China, Mongolia, Japan everywhere with scholars from different disciplines to study all interaction from food to culture to religion to architecture, everything.

First, I discovered something which was not well-known, the very ancient presence of Afro-descendants in Asia. They were the explorers who left [the] African continent thousands of years ago and went to the Asian continent and the Chinese archeologists during my expeditions in China while I was there with all the most competent modern equipment. They did show us some place and they're telling us, "Doudou, we have discovered an African kingdom here, the remnants of a kingdom that they left."

David: Fascinating.

Doudou: Secondly, it was discovered UNESCO on the civilization on the Indus Valley which as you know was one of the most fascinating civilizations as you know was destroyed in 2500 BC millennium, long time ago. It was when that civilization was destroyed, what is called now Pakistan in the Indus Valley. When the people were living in the Indus Valley in the cities of Mohenjo-Daro and Harappa which are very sophisticated cities, moved down to the sub-continent and was the first inhabitants of India. They're now from the middle of India to Sri Lanka; as you know they're all black.

The origin of Indian civilization it isn't now being completely recognized is the Elamo-Dravidian and as you know the most loved God of Hinduism, Krishna, Krishna means black.

David: Is that right? I did not know that.

Doudou: Yes, it is black, what it means in Telugu, in Dravidian language and now still black, dark. As you know in the painting, traditional painting, it is painted so dark that they call it blue.

David: Yes.

Doudou: What I'm saying is that historical Africans went to Asia and they have marked very profoundly, spiritually, culturally all the Asian nations. We are now promoting and studies are being conducted etcetera. I can give you more information about it.

Secondly, in my work of the Slave Route, and in my work as a special reporter of racism I did evidently investigate all the Western hemisphere, the Caribbean and South America. I discovered that as an Afro-descendant in those parts of the Western hemisphere did profoundly transform and mark all their surroundings, now cultural and natural. Their cultures are the main pillar until now of the culture of the Western hemisphere. They keep reinventing, inventing, transforming their environment in a process of re-humanizing themselves, but also of resistance.

This is why as you know all the cultures of the Americas and the Caribbean's are so profoundly marked by the Afro-descendants' powerful expression of culture and spirituality. Evidently, it is a case in the United States. I respond by telling you that a few years ago, Le Monde, which is one of the main newspapers in France ...published in the front page... an article saying, "The Black culture dominates the world." It was very convincing for many people and the analysis was that the black culture, African culture not only in the African continent, but also in the Americas are so powerful in their expressions because they're a very powerful link between material, the spiritual and artistic mixture that they have transformed all the environment where they have been living.

My conclusion that we have now a golden opportunity to document all this transformation. As you know, the UN has adopted last year the UN Decade of Afro-descendants. I was active in the process of getting the UN to approve this during the assembly and I'm still very active now in implementation. It will last until 2024. Now all the Afro-descendants in the Americas, in Europe, in Asia are now mobilizing themselves, not only to identify themselves, organize themselves, but assess their situation historically and in the socioeconomic presently.

Now we have a powerful opportunity and a golden opportunity.... The time has come to move Afro-descendants in the Americas and in Europe and elsewhere in Asia from the position of victims to the position of force of transformation of the societies where they are living, because Afro-descendants cannot remain, accept and be locked in the ghetto of victim, because it is part of the ideology of construction of racism.

[The] UN Decade of Afro-descendants is a golden opportunity to assess ... Afro-descendants in the Americas. We are now in the middle of the very powerful process of change.

David: Outstanding, that's outstanding. Well, we hope that certainly the book that we intend to publish in the beginning of next year will bring even greater attention to this decade and to this constant struggle and the globalization of this struggle through your efforts and others. We hope that we can contribute, in some way. We're just helping you to spread the word, because as I'm sure you know, too, the African American sense of world affairs has been, I think part of the construct of racism. It has been limited and many that live in and among the various cities here in the United States don't really see themselves as world citizens yet. I think that what you're doing is important to begin to make those bridges happen.

Doudou: Yes, exactly. You know I will tell you David, because every day now, every week [there are] meetings, meetings somewhere of Afro-descendants to organize themselves. One of the last meetings was in Rotterdam, Netherlands three weeks ago with European Afro-descendants. They got together and they invited me to give the keynote speech and be a part of the discussion. I will send you the summary of my presentation. It is short where you will see some of the main ideas I expressed. Now what

I would like to add to the point you made is that one of the reasons why Afro-descendants in the United States had difficulty in getting out of the slavery mantle system is that the system has been built on the strategy divide to divide Afro-descendants and to cut their link with Africa first by saying that Africans are responsible of their enslavement.

[The system of slavery] depicted Africans as kind of wild and not civilized people. What I'm saying is that the ideology of racism has been so subtle and so profound that for a long time it has put in the mind set of Afro-descendants in the Americas the idea that they were different from Africans. As you know, because of the intellectual fight of personalities of Marcus Garvey, Martin Luther King, Malcolm X, all of them have really put the necessary to relink with Africa and to get back to the African root and have elaborated the ideas the fight of Afro-descendants is a continuity from Africa to the Americas to Europe and to different parts of the world. That was expressed powerfully by intellectuals like James Baldwin and others and slowly the reuniting of Africans and Afro-descendants [is] becoming a reality. This is one of the most important new frontiers of the come-back of the Afro-descendants, to give substance and meaning as their linkage with Africa.

Now I must say that Africa is responding, certainly slowly, but very powerfully because as you know the African union has decided that Afro-descendants will be considered as a kind of last 51st state of Africa. That they constitute a kind of symbolic community as part of that African continent and that African writers, singers, actors, are very powerful, being inspired by the history of Afro-descendant in the Americas.

We are now in the middle of this process, but one dimension ... we have to combat [is] we have to understand that our fight is universal. When we are talking about Afro-descendants certainly in the recent history the situation of the Afro-descendant in the Americas is a very dramatic and important dimension, because it is a fight of Afro-descendants in the Americas and Caribbean [and] people in the Americas who have been contributing to this still.

It is certainly true that color has been a factor, that using color as an expression of identity has been a dimension [to] also fight back to say, "Yes we are proud of our color."

We have to integrate that dimension of diversity in the Afro-descendant community and refuse the colorism in which they have tried to lock us. This point is highly important for us and an expression of this is that we have to understand that when we are talking about Afro- descendants we have to know that there are millions of Afro-descendants in India, in the Pacific Islands, in Australia, even in Russia.

Doudou: As you know, the most important poet of Russia, the man most loved by Russian culture is Alexander Pushkin—who's a descendant of [an] enslaved man in the Russian empire. This universal dimension is another frontier which we have to document, confront and organize and which leaders who make the Afro-descendant the most important force in the twenty-first century, to transfer to make a reality of all societies as multicultural societies. All societies have been the result of these very profound changes. At the heart of these changes throughout the history … of Afro-descendants has been the very fundamental dimension.

This is why I am insisting on the need [for] the new party to transform [the] Afro-descendant from a situation of victim… to the situation of powerful force of the transformation of change of the societies where they are living. All the fronts will be confronted. Certainly the social economic and political front, but also the cultural and the spiritual front linking them all, as the history of Afro-descendants [has] demonstrated.

David: Outstanding; very profound, very profound. This is wonderful, Doudou Diène. Let me guide it a bit further. You mentioned Baldwin and Malcolm and Dr. King and several other African American leaders. You obviously have studied and are very aware of their contributions. Let me ask in your opinion is there one or two of those individuals that influenced your thinking and that had, some of them, a very important impact on the course of thinking and study that you're undertaking?

Doudou: Oh clearly, no doubt. All of us people of my generation, when we started being engaged with our elders in the fight against colonization, first we started as you know to engage against colonization [of] society on the intellectual front. Immediately, you have to know that the figures of Marcus Garvey, Malcolm X, Martin Luther King, James Baldwin immersed very strongly in the African freedom fighters.

They were integrated, read, quoted as a force, [an] intellectual force. This has been part of my life and all our elders…. [W]hen you listen … to the artistic expression of Africans now in the continent, not only in the field of music, but art, sculpture, you will see that those figures of Afro-descendants in the Americas have profoundly inspired the new generation of African intellectuals and artists in a very profound way.

David: Now I'm going to ask, it might be a difficult question to capture in just a few thoughts, but I want you to try to think of a specific moment or period in the past four hundred years of the African American experience here in the States that stands out as being uniquely important. Now understanding, of course, that it's all a continuum and that is not lost on me, but if there were one or perhaps two moments in the experience here of this country of descendants of Africa, what would you say?

Doudou: [T]here is no doubt in our memory and deep in our heart the figure of Martin Luther King. I listened again to Martin Luther King's speech in Washington, my eyes just started to water. I am so deeply moved and this I think is one incredible moment; but one thing I would like to tell you and answer the question, the struggle of Afro-descendants, African Americans, the main force, has certainly been individuals who carry it over and [who] will get visibility and [have] history capture their name and the image.

It was anonymous work, done daily as I said earlier by women in the plantation in the evening when they tried to strengthen the vitality of enslaved who came back from the plantation, their body completely broken.

That daily struggle I think makes the history of Afro-descendants not the history of individuals, but a collective history because it is the strength, the resilience throughout centuries of the anonymous daily work, fight of Afro-descendants which in my view should make them the anonymous heroes of this struggle which is continuing. Which is the same that African Americans living in Chicago, in Miami, in New York facing the police brutality, fighting to get places of Congress in the visibility of the media.

David: Excellent, excellent. Well you've touched already a bit on the final question, but let's explore it a bit more, given that there seems to be among many scholars that they agree that this is a pivotal point right now in American history certainly, but in global history as well. In that many of the gains that were fought for, for so long seemed to be being challenged by the power structure and the power elite. My question on this is what insights, opinions or perspectives would you give to African Americans in this era as they continue the struggle to repel racism to maintain these gains that have been so hard won and perhaps most importantly find footage and advancement going forward? What would you say to our readers

Doudou: I will say two things David. The first point is to remind everybody that one of the ideological and psychological strategies of those who created enslavement from the European thinkers, to those who implemented them in the Americas is to let us believe that racism is something you cannot combat, that it is part of the natural reality. It is like the sun, like the moon, like the sky, that there is no way we can combat it. This is why I personally insist everywhere I speak and... when I launched [the] Slave Route program in UNESCO to remind everybody that racism is an intellectual, social and political construction based on the power and strategy of domination. That construction can be deconstructed and that every thumb of racism, be it racism against [the] Black man, be it anti-Semitism, be it Islamophobia, you can get their beginning, you can retrace their origin. You can deconstruct their language and you can identify their social, political and economic expression. This point is very important: racism is a social, political and cultural construction that can be fought. This is important because it will give hope to victims [of] racism that, yes, they can fight it back.

Secondly, all the historic African Americans showed this ...because they keep fighting; they keep fighting every day, every minute, against policy, against violence, against all tangible violence and they succeeded. Certainly, that every gain will be challenged not only by the system, but even negated by some African Americans themselves who don't recognize the gain. Because [of] the fact that some African Americans in their own mind they have said, Yes there's nothing you can do against the system. It's part of the ideology of that domination.

This is why it's important to link the situation of Afro-descendants in the Americas to the situation of Afro-descendants in India, in the Pacific, in Europe, etcetera and to give it a universal dimension. Things are changing very profoundly, but one expression of the very profound depth of ideology of racism is to let us believe that nothing has changed, there is nothing you can do. It is not true.

David: Outstanding. Well, Doudou, you have been tremendous, tremendous. I'm very excited about your input and we are as always brothers in the struggle with you. We support all your amazing work. We hope that this piece will add to it.

INDIA

l-r Dr. Shashi Tharoor, Under Secretary of the UN for Communications and Public Information;
UN Secretary General Kofi Annan; Alice Palmer; Edward "Buzz" Palmer

1. Shashi Tharoor

Shashi Tharoor, born 9 March 1956, is an Indian politician and a former diplomat, who is currently serving as a member of parliament, Lok Sabha from Thiruvananthapuram, Kerala since 2009. He also currently serves as chairman of the Parliamentary Standing Committee on External Affairs and All India Professionals Congress of the Indian National Congress.

He was previously minister of state in the government of India for External Affairs (2009–2010) and Human Resource Development (2012–2014). Until 2007, he was a career official at the United Nations, rising to the rank of undersecretary general for communications and public information in 2001. He announced his retirement after finishing second in the 2006 selection for U.N. secretary-general to Ban Ki-moon.

Tharoor is also an acclaimed writer, having authored sixteen bestselling works of fiction and non-fiction since 1981, all of which are centered on India and its history, culture, film, politics, society, foreign policy, and more. He is also the author of hundreds of columns and articles in publications such as *The New York Times, The Washington Post, TIME Magazine, Newsweek,* and *The Times of India.* Tharoor is a globally recognized speaker on India's economics and politics, as well as on freedom of the press, human rights, Indian culture, and international affairs.

"I Felt a Strong Affinity for the Struggles and Achievements of Black Americans"

I met Black Americans for the first time when I came to the United States as a graduate student in 1975. There were a handful in my class at the Fletcher School of Law & Diplomacy; but then our class, too, was small, just 99 of us from over thirty countries. The peripatetic nature of my working life has meant that contact with all my Fletcher classmates, irrespective of ethnicity, has been largely sporadic, but I'm proud that I've been in touch with some of those friends into the third decade after our graduation, two of whom have been African American.

I left the United States in 1978 to join the United Nations in Geneva and knew several Africans, but no African Americans, during my postings there and in Southeast Asia. But when I returned to the United States in 1989 to serve at UN Headquarters and live in New York, I naturally got to know a large cross-section of Americans, many of whom were Black American. Some became close friends—and one whom I am regularly in touch with by email, practically daily, is the inspiration for this volume, Professor Edward "Buzz" Palmer.

For some of us, the "Americanness" of Black Americans is a more obvious feature than their "blackness", and so we see then essentially as American. "Black" becomes an adjective describing the kind of American they are, rather than part of a compound noun defining them as equally Black and American. For others—those who, for whatever cultural or political reason, are more conscious of color—it's the blackness they notice first that gives them the lens through which they see the Black Americans they meet. In my years living around the world, I found that many dark-skinned people hardly saw Black Americans as black; their Americanness differentiated them too starkly from other black people, especially Africans.

The question of social acceptance of Black Americans varies not only from country to country, but within foreign countries. Educated, cosmopolitan people with wide exposure to the world tend to be more accepting than those whose prejudices against foreigners are more easily stoked up, and sometimes compounded by issues of race. Africans in India, for instance, have seen the entire gamut of local reactions, from being welcomed in a spirit of solidarity and goodwill by many, to being attacked by a few as criminals and worse principally because of their skin color. I have not heard from enough Black Americans whether their own experiences in India were comparable to their African counterparts.

Among educated people across the world, there is widespread admiration for what Black Americans have accomplished, overcoming a legacy of slavery and discrimination to carve a place for themselves in American society. Working at the United Nations, I felt a strong affinity for their struggle and accomplishments.

Some years ago, I was fascinated to read in an article about Harlem, the most vibrant neighborhood in the city that has given the United Nations its home, a paragraph that read:

> "There is a perception that no more than two feet separate church and state at the Abyssinian Baptist Church in Harlem. The short distance between the preacher and his pulpit inside the [now nearly a century]-old gothic fortress has been a gray area between politics and religion since the church's inception. From flamboyant lawmaker Adam Clayton Powell Jr. to fiery orator Calvin Butts, the church has long been associated with political as well as spiritual guidance."

So, it was a special honor indeed for me to have been invited by the "fiery orator", Reverend Butts, to address the Abyssinian Baptist Church one Sunday morning in 2003. I was proud, too, to represent there a man who knew both Africa and America well, Kofi Annan. To Black Americans I was able to say with conviction that the United Nations is us; it is you and me.

Black Americans were, for me, natural allies of the UN. Much of what the UN seeks to do requires rousing the consciences of the affluent and tranquil about the plight of the poor and the strife-torn. Large sections of the world's people require desperately-needed help from the United Nations to surmount problems they cannot overcome on their own.

The world continues to face (to use Kofi Annan's phrase) innumerable "problems without passports" — problems of the proliferation of weapons of mass destruction, of the degradation of our common environment, of contagious disease and chronic starvation, of human rights and human wrongs, of mass illiteracy and massive displacement. These are problems that no one country, however powerful, can solve on its own, and which are yet the shared responsibility of humankind. And they are problems that echo many that Black Americans have themselves overcome. They cry out for solutions that, like the problems themselves, also cross frontiers—and that was what gave us at the United Nations an affinity for the travails of Black Americans. "The rest," to quote the memorable phrase of a distinguished member of that community, E.R. Shipp, "is hamburger history."

The UN was born of the same impulses that gave the world the historic African-Asian summit in Bandung, Indonesia, in 1955. Adam Clayton Powell and Margaret Cartwright, the first African American reporter assigned to the United Nations, were present at that conference. They saw early on the vital importance of connecting with nations around the world, many of whom had emerged from experiences of colonial oppression that African Americans could understand and relate to.

This was why I believed, and argued, that African Americans were natural allies of the United Nations. The NAACP's Walter White, the great man of letters W.E.B. DuBois, and Mary McLeod Bethune were observers at the San Francisco conference that created the UN. Their activism was vital in infusing into the UN Charter many of its most precious ideals of equality and human values.

But let me go beyond that. In the words of Ralph Bunche, perhaps the most distinguished American to serve the UN, "If you want to get across an idea, wrap it up in a person." Let me wrap this idea up in Ralph Bunche. One of the greatest figures associated with the United Nations, Ralph Bunche was also an African American, who founded Howard University's political science department.

During Kofi Annan's years as head of United Nations peacekeeping, he always kept a picture of Bunche on his wall, hoping to gain courage and inspiration from his life and work. From his days as a star at UCLA to his Ph.D. at Harvard, to his pioneering work as a researcher in race studies and civil rights, Bunche was destined for greatness. And he put his extraordinary abilities at the service of world peace. From Cyprus to Kashmir to the Congo to the Middle East, Bunche worked tirelessly for peace and justice. It was for his historic role making peace in Palestine that Bunche was awarded the Nobel Peace Prize in 1950. In his acceptance speech,

Bunche declared that "the United Nations exists not merely to preserve the peace but also to make change—even radical change—possible without violent upheaval."

Bunche is today less well-known around the world than the greatest American advocate of change without violence, Martin Luther King. More than sixty years ago he declared that "our world is geographically one. Now we are faced with [the] challenge of making it spiritually one. Through our scientific genius we have made of the world of a neighborhood; now, through moral and spiritual genius, we must make of it a brotherhood."

His foresight was extraordinary. Dr. King saw that the global village presents us with an ethical challenge: to seek to ensure that human progress is matched by human understanding. A remarkable thing about Dr. King was that he could describe the world in 1957 in the same way that we might describe our global village in 2017. But the question that comes back to us today remains: How can what we dare to describe as a global village, learn to act as a global brotherhood?

The United Nations Declaration of Human Rights has been a fundamental source of inspiration for national and international efforts to protect and promote human rights and freedoms. Conceived as a "common standard of achievements for all peoples and all nations", the Declaration has become a yardstick by which to measure progress towards full equality for African Americans in the United States as well as the respect for, and compliance with, international human rights standards abroad.

The first article of the Declaration is quite simple: "All human beings are born free and equal in dignity and rights. They are endowed with reason and conscience and should act towards one another in a spirit of brotherhood." Brotherhood: there is that word again. That first article, like Dr. King's words, is no less true, no less relevant and no less important today. As the first Black American president of the United States leaves office, it is sad that so many of his fellow men and women in America believe their place in American society is more under threat than before.

Barack Obama exemplified so much that the world admired about America: he became an emblem of opportunity, of openness to the world, of equal rights for all and of decency and human values infusing a position of power. But as he steps out of the White House, has it become a "White" house again in every sense of the term?

Obama's ascent enhanced the stature of Americans generally, and Black Americans particularly, around the world. If Dr. King's Nobel Prize seemed to mark the moment when Black Americans truly received worldwide acceptance, Obama's election and re-election stand out for me as the most significant moment in four hundred years of Black American history. His personal manner ensured that Black Americans were never disparaged as a community abroad; certainly I have never heard an expression like "Ugly American" being applied to a Black American.

People in many countries, especially ethnic minorities, are inspired by King and Obama to fight for racial justice and to believe their ethnicity will not prevent their rise to the top. Fondness for African American culture abroad may begin and end with jazz and rap, and familiarity with Black Americans may not extend beyond basketball players and entertainers, but prejudice is largely absent in most international narratives.

Since I am an Indian writer, allow me to end with an Indian story—a tale from our ancient scriptures, the Puranas. It is a typical Indian story of a sage and his disciples. The sage asks his disciples, "When does the night end?" And the disciples say, "At dawn, of course." The sage says, "I know that. But when does the night end and the dawn begin?" The first disciple, who is from the tropical south of India, where I come from, replies: "When the first glimmer of light across the sky reveals the palm fronds on the coconut trees swaying in the breeze, that is when the night ends and the dawn begins." The sage says "No," so the second disciple, who is from the cold north, ventures: "When the first streaks of sunshine make the snow gleam white on the mountaintops of the Himalayas, that is when the night ends and the dawn begins." The sage says, "No, my sons. When two travelers from opposite ends of our land meet and embrace each other as brothers, and when they realize they sleep under the same sky, see the same stars and dream the same dreams—that is when the night ends and the dawn begins."

There has been many a dark night for the world in the millennium that has just passed. Whether as Indians, as African Americans, or just plain Americans, we are citizens of the world, and brothers and sisters in it. There is one world, after all, and it is ours. It is only by realizing this that all of us can work to ensure that the world can enjoy a new dawn in the next one. And, in that spirit, let us keep the faith.

2. Ramu Damodaran

Ramu Damodaran is deputy director for partnerships and public engagement in the United Nations Department of Public Information's Outreach Division. He previously served as chief of its Civil Society Service.

His earlier assignments with the organization have included the departments of Peacekeeping and Special Political Questions as well as the Executive Office of the Secretary-General. He served as secretary of the Secretary-General's mission to Kuwait in 1991, following the invasion by Iraq, and as spokesperson for the Durban Review Conference, held in Geneva in 2009. While a member of the Indian Foreign Service, he served as executive assistant to the prime minister of India from 1991 to 1994. He has also served in the Indian diplomatic missions in Moscow and at the United Nations and in assignments in New Delhi with a range of governmental ministries including External Affairs, Home Affairs, Defense, Planning and Human Resource Development.

Prior to joining national government service, he worked extensively in Indian mass media, including television, radio and print publications, as a news anchor and disc jockey.

Interview by David Robinson by phone

My Father Spoke to Me of DuBois

David: If you wouldn't mind telling me your name and spelling of the name so that we can make sure we have everything right.

Ramu: Right. The first name is Ramu, R-A-M-U. And the last name is Damodaran, which is D-A-M-O-D-A-R-A-N.

David: Excellent. Well, thank you. So, let's get going. What first brought you in contact with Black Americans in your work? Or in your life, actually?

Ramu: I actually grew up... I was in a foreign service family. My father was in foreign service. And, I do recall that when we were in Germany in the sixties, in Berlin, I did have an African American classmate at what was then called the

John F. Kennedy School. I remember his name. It was Tim but unfortunately we only had about eight months or so together because in the way of all diplomatic families, sadly my parents were reassigned and we moved on to China. But, what really struck me about him was that he was the first person through whom I discovered the world of American comics, at that stage—including Dennis the Menace and Archie. There was a store in Berlin which was really meant for American servicemen to which he and his family visited often. And, so he used to buy these comics and bring them and share them with us. So it became my window into American culture, or the United States culture, at that point in time. I must have been... What was I? About seven or so. It was through this African American student that American culture was introduced to me at that point.

David: How interesting. Now, Dennis the Menace, Archie... I used to read all those comics, too, and I recall noticing at some point that there were very few people of color in any of those comic books. Did that occur to you as a very young lad as well?

Ramu: Now that you mention it, yes. I mean, I think that there were...it was quite clear because he was probably also the first American I knew, quite possibly, the first African American because until my parents moved to Berlin I had been in local schools. I was in a German school in Bonn and a Czech school in Prague. So this was my first so called international school and he was the only African American in our class. So, it was quite clear that... The picture of America, of course, was in many ways that of actors we'd see on film. And, of course, John F. Kennedy who was the president while we were in Bonn back here in '63. So the idea all through these comics really seemed a very important book in America, considering that they were introduced to me by someone who was African American had its own impact; but I must say in all honesty I don't ever recall discussing this aspect, nor his raising it.

David: Interesting. Excellent. Yeah, very ironic introduction, wouldn't you say, to the culture? Let me ask, what would you say is the level of interest in black culture in your country? You mentioned Archie and kind of very typical sort of fifties TV inspired culture. When did you first recognize that there was an entirely differently culture in the African American community?

Ramu: At the point that really struck me, and I think it struck a lot of people in

India, was that a few years after my time in Berlin, when I moved back to Delhi and then…. I want to say it was sometime in '67 or '68 that the Sidney Poitier film To Sir, With Love played in Delhi.

David: Yes.

Ramu: And that really took a lot of people… It engaged a lot of people because [it was a] powerful and endearing film, but also because of the situation that it pictured. So that was one key opening of experience to me. The other was when I was studying at the Jesuit school. One of the priests there, who happened to be an American, a white American from Chicago, lent me a book whose name I'll not forget. It was called, Black Like Me.

David: Ah. Yes, yes. Yes.

Ramu: You are probably familiar with that book.

David: Absolutely. Yes.

Ramu: That again was something which exposed me to it but I think more important than that, I was… I mentioned that I came from a foreign service family but more important, as far as my father was concerned, is that he tried to be, prior to the service, he was very much involved in India's own national movement and the freedom struggle. He was very involved in that aspect of our history and he brought to light two important connections which he used to talk to me about. One, of course, was the connection with Du Bois.

David: Yes.

Ramu: And, the fact that in India we have a community of people who are underprivileged who Mahatma Gandhi called God's children and these are people who now have protection under our constitution and they had a leader called Dr. Ambedkar. And, I recall my father telling me how soon after the United Nations began, I think probably 1946 or 1947, Dr. Ambedkar wrote a letter to Du Bois asking him for his guidance of how the situation of the balance… We call it the AFIT in India could be called before the United Nations in the same way that Dr. Du Bois had tried to bring the problems of the African Americans before the United Nations. I think Dr. Du Bois was, at that point, in Atlanta and Sidney Poitier in Atlanta. And this was a connection between them. In the event what really happened… And I'm looking back to my present United Nations career, is that despite the fact that the United

Nations speak as entities. In other words, it's not communities within the United States or communities within India, but the human race. I think one thing, for people like Du Bois and Dr. Ambedkar, which led to some of our most important international agreements, including the protection of the rules against discrimination and the fact that we have many to deal with the situation of minorities, but that's something I should probably elaborate on later.

To go back to your questions about India, the other person who is much less well known in a sense but whom my father mentioned as someone who was important was a person called Cedric Dover. Now, Cedric Dover was... He is... I think he is one of the expats living in Europe but was from India and he was born in Calcutta in India. And then moved on to Europe after studying in India and wrote a wonderful book called "Half Caste" thinking about race and color. And, soon after India developed in 1947, he moved to the United States where again he began to work on Anthropology but his focus was on minority communities in the United States and he was at a university called Fisk and then here at the new school in New York and then at Howard University in Washington.

David: Fascinating.

Ramu: And he was really remarkable for, as someone born in India and with no connection at all to the United States or to the African American community, coming to that community from the sanctity and perspective of an anthropologist, then moving on [to] the cultural studies in America and then being able to travel back and bring that to India. But, of course, the third individual all of us knew in India was Paul Robeson. And this was not only because of his own personal excellence, but because he met a wonderful Indian musician from East India, from the state of Arifar, a man called Bhuben Hazarika.... And Bhuben Hazarika, who passed on a few years ago, translated "Old Man River" into both Hindi and another local language. And, so that became part of the Indian musical creation as well. Just as another part, which can often be easily identified with the African American community in its origins which really became at... of the Civil Rights movement and that is "We Shall Overcome."

David: Yes. Yes.

Ramu: That was translated into several Indian languages. It's one of the... It's, in many ways, one of the easiest songs to translate because of the syllable count. We...shall...over...come... from this it was not very difficult to transfer this into the syllable counts in Hindi. I think that captured much imagination. It was very much admired in India.

David: Fascinating. You know, Ramu, these are hidden bits of history that we often don't hear in this country, and certainly in my community. Normally, the discussion about relationships between East Indians and African Americans is...often starts with Howard Thurman and his visits with Gandhi and others. And, then, Howard Thurman convincing Dr. Martin Luther King to go and visit and learn about non-violent protests.

Ramu: Mm-hmm.

David: So, what you shared brings in a much greater context to that process. So, that's very, very exciting. I appreciate that. And, outside the U.S... Oh, I'm sorry, let me go back a question here. In your country, do you believe Black Americans are generally regarded with admiration, disdain or indifference and why or why not?

Ramu: I think it's always difficult to conceptualize India in a single statement. India is so vast and varied and there are parts of India which are very aligned to external experiences like the African American because they're very aware and they've watched a great deal, they've listened to a great deal. So they're much more knowledgeable. In other parts of India, the knowledge is more technically unaware. But actually the one factor which unites all of India is everyone in India ... has faced some form of, let's say clearly some form of oppression and discrimination, whether through the process of colonization or the process of being traumatized on the basis of your color or your ethnic background. And so there's a great affinity, and I use that word particularly because I do not want to use the word sympathy which is, I think, much less accurate. There's a great affinity in every Indian with every citizen of another country who have undergone the same degree of discrimination. Whose community has had, in many ways, a more difficult time of acquiring or securing their rights than other communities have. So I think there's an inbuilt ability, perhaps even in many cases a profound similarity.

David: Fascinating. Excellent. You spoke earlier of Paul Robeson and Du Bois and some others who were very instrumental early in the struggle here in this country.

Ramu: Yes.

David: Moving forward, are there other recognized Black Americans that have had impact or have emerged as important in India in arts, literature, music, justice, politics? Let's carry it forward a few decades and I want to get a sense if you hear of any of that discussion in India. Are there certain people that you recognize later that made a difference or had some impact?

Ramu: Certainly the entire music experience with the West has been substantially African American. Whether you think of jazz or vocal music or even, for that matter, the folk or classical music and so on. You have the entire industry of jazz like Louis Armstrong, for instance. You have music popular in ballrooms like Duke Ellington. You have the music like that of Nat King Cole in the sixties. Today's styles, whether it's Stevie Wonder or Jay Z or people that are in popular music. And then you go beyond that to the other arts where I think it becomes a little more anonymous. So I don't want to exaggerate the degree of affinity that there is, but I do wish to project that it's now become, for want of a better word, noble. So there's nothing unexpected in finding a great talent one admires, whether it be the creative arts, the musical arts or the cinematic arts, who is from the African American community because it's become much, much easier and talent is recognized and is shared. And I think that's been the Indian experience within India.

David: Excellent. Interesting. On a related note, moving more toward politics and global affairs, are there any African American leaders—current leaders— that you would say have had some impact or people pay attention to in India?

Ramu: It's difficult to answer this question without getting into sensitive local politics, but I think, without question, the Obama election in the United States has captured the Indian imagination because of the individual and the historic nature of the results. I feel that, in many ways, the fact of the community from which it comes is not a defining factor, but something that is inherited in that community and the history the community feels within that community and all he has expressed as a human being and his presentation as the leader he is. So I think that goes without saying. Again, by and large, I think Indians... having lived in New York for almost twenty-five years now, I am aware of prominent African American political, judicial, intellectual leaders in this country. I think they're probably less well known in India but again, as I tried to say earlier, I don't think there would be the remotest element of surprise in discovering that the people whom one reads about or whom one admires actually are from the African American community. And you mentioned the fact, you know, you mentioned the name of Howard Thurman a little while ago and I think that, in a sense, was very...is very emblematic because if you look back to his meetings with Mahatma Gandhi the one thing that stood out about that was he had a wonderful faith there about life, living about life, which he shared with Gandhi. And I think that's especially true to, you know, to respond to your Indian question, that lives are no longer distinct or separate or measured by ethnic background. It's really life upon life in the sense of community that one looks to. And there, I think, everyone in India recognizes the vibrant philosophy in this and the contribution of the African American community.

David: That's actually quite beautiful, that thought, isn't it?

Ramu: Yeah, I think so. Very powerful, yeah.

David: In your opinion, is there a specific moment or period in the past four hundred years or so of African American history that stands out as being uniquely important or compelling in some way, to you?

Ramu: I don't know enough about eighteenth to nineteenth century American history. My knowledge, both in terms of formal study at school and college and in terms of reading, has really been the twentieth century. I can be supremely moved and inspired by what people say, so when I read a speech of someone like, say, Abraham Lincoln to go back to the nineteenth century, it has a power over me which, you know, the majesty as well as the brutality of the Civil War. And then you come into the twentieth century and the increasing engagement of the United States, not only in world affairs, but...openly, publicly and democratically dealing with its own important issues. I was very fortunate to see two very major museums—one in Atlanta and the other in New Orleans—which really traced the Civil Rights movement and both of them made a deep impression on me. And, I think what... I think the two enduring thoughts that connect with me was the fact that everyone who's not just young muscular men... At the time there were women, there were children, there were Asian shop keepers who took part in that movement and rallied. You have, whether it's marching, or boycotting, or beyond that, apart from the historical images of resistance and so on. So that is one example of how the United States offers the opportunity for people to come together within a sovereign country and protest their cause. And, on the other hand, there's the fact that it is also a country which allowed, through the process of freedom of expression and speech, the most vicious form of bigotry to the most basic and political level, even in terms of the institutional level to the individual level. And so, I think, those two things together in the one country, or the one dominant point of these four hundred years that you have been struggling for equality is the fact that, ultimately, this country allows all points of view to be expressed, no matter how horrific, no matter how unimaginable, or for that matter how desperate. And, through that process, is able to work out a system that is just and fair to all and I think that's remarkable.

David: That is indeed remarkable and I think Mr. Jefferson and Mr. Franklin and his colleagues would really appreciate that you, from a country quite far away, have embraced the ideals that were written in some of the founding language of this country. And, the struggle to achieve those quite lofty goals, is a continuing process and, hopefully, we're making some progress. But, the fact that the essence of those words and those ideals has moved you, and one can only hope that given the current political structure and economic structure here in this country, that seems to have moved away from, I think, the spirit of that language. They would do well to read this section in our book that you have noted. So...

Ramu: Thank you.

David: This last question requires a little bit of background and I suspect that, in your work, you are probably very uniquely aware of this, but many scholars now see this period that we're living in as a pivotal point in modern history, as a global and political economy shifting. American hedge money is being challenged and many nations and cultures once considered undeveloped, including India some years ago, are coming to the forefront. While there's no question Black Americans have been vital to the political, economic and social development in these United States from its inception, even when those words were written, to some degree, going forward Black Americans seem to be at risk of remaining or becoming more marginalized as racial prejudice and poverty continue to kind of be very stubbornly in place. And other ethnic groups are also fighting for their share of America's shrinking base of resources. We've consistently, in the Black American community, benefited from relationships and dialogue with other countries. And you eluded to that with Robeson, with the visits of various scholars and peace makers over the last one hundred years. The question now, though, is what insights, opinions or perspectives would you give to African Americans that might read this book and are grappling with all this uncertainty? What would suggest to help continue the struggle to repel racism, to maintain some of the hard won gains and, perhaps most importantly, figure ways to advance going forward? How would you feel you were able to speak to all of us, what might you say?

Ramu: It would be very presumptuous of me to speak to any group of people in the sense of giving just sort of council or advice on how to conduct themselves, but... So, let me phrase it a little differently. Rather than specify something for the African American community in particular, I think from both a national and an international point of view, any community that seeks an identity, or sees an identity should be able to work, I think, at two levels. One is to protect perhaps the first identity in cultural terms, in terms of language, in terms of manifestations such as food.

Ramu: But, at the other level, the largest common identity to which one belongs, whether it is American or Indian, or for that matter, ultimately global. And, so when one can come to terms with that, then you realize that identities are not a form of retreat but, actually a form of assertion for first moving forward. You have to protect your identity. You have the responsibility to protect and nurture your identity of which you are proud and that you want to share with the world. But, at the same time, it's not something [that] constrains you. You are part of a larger whole and if we are able to do this, whether it is minorities or majorities, or the disadvantaged or advantaged, I think it would help people embrace their uniqueness and their human sameness. That's much better. I've often thought of the metaphor, which

I think that maybe you will know the name, but I forget the name, is a spiritual African American leader who had an essay from early in the twentieth century and he said that, whenever I go to mail a letter in a mailbox I always look to see whether, on the handle, it says "pull down" or whether it says "lift up." And that's really the difference. Are you going to as a community feel, that because of history and because of circumstance, you are going to remain and pull down or are you, because of the courage that you have displayed and the fact that you are part of a larger and more hopeful whole, are you going to lift up?

David: Outstanding. I must say, Ramu, that I have conducted several of these interviews now and, typically, they go for more than an hour and partly because, and nothing against the people that I've interviewed, but the clarity of expression and the certain lyricism that you possess that allowed us to get through the questions in remarkably quick time, but with a great amount of profound insight. And I really appreciate that. Your answers were so profoundly insightful and articulated in such a way that there's a bit of music about them and I really appreciate that.

Ramu: Thanks so much, David.

David: Well, those are the questions. Do you have any additional thoughts that you might want to share? On this topic or any others?

Ramu: No, I think the only thing which I should like to say, which I've not been able to, reflects back to something from the beginning about how Dr. DuBois had wanted to bring the African Americans to the United Nations and while it did not seem as a subject in itself, it has been assimilated in a large number of new instruments and documents that have been inspired by the African American experience and cause. But, going from that fact that, maybe thanks to the work of Buzz and Alice and yourself and the … program in Chicago, the fact that the United Nations was able to engage with African American civil society, with African American business leaders, with African American religious leaders, the trip to the United Nations, had them talk with each other, with United Nations officials, I think is a tribute first of all to Alice and Buzz, second to the community itself and third I think... to the United Nations of America which is secure enough in its domestic arrangements and politics as not to be offended or wounded if any particular community in this country comes to the United Nations and joins or offers support or discussion. And that's something which I think is only natural in a country that was really close to the creation of the United Nations and is a host to the United Nations as a partner in 2016.

David: Excellent. Yes, I recall I was at, I think, the first gathering of that group.

Ramu: Right.

David: And it was a remarkable experience, you know. It was a tremendous opportunity and many of our guests tend to still speak very highly of that opportunity. Particularly meeting with Secretary Anan and being able to kind of be part of the global community in such a close and intimate way was, I think, very inspiring for people.

Ramu: Thank you for that, David.

David: Excellent. Well, this concludes the official interview...So, thank you so much, Ramu.

Ramu: Thank you, David. And take care. Bye.

David: You too. Goodbye now.

SINGAPORE

1. Shantoba Eliza Carew-Edwin

Shantoba Eliza Carew-Edwin, MA, MS, is the founder of Turning Globe Tuition Ltd (TGT), which is a higher education consulting firm that pairs multicultural students with educational opportunities in the United States and other parts of the world. Turning Globe Tuition draws attention to more diverse populations of highly-motivated students who might otherwise not have the same access to top-tier institutions. Since moving to Singapore, she has extended her skills in bringing people together—this time in the arts—by taking on the position of business and operations manager of Little Artists Art Studio.

I Have Often Felt Like a Black Pioneer

I have lived outside of the United States permanently since 2008 and this includes: 6 months in Austria; 18 months in Sweden; 2 years in France; 3 years in London, England; and now almost 3 years in Singapore, where I still live with my husband. I always wanted to live abroad, particularly in Europe or Asia—Europe for the castles and Asia for business—one fanciful step back into history, one leap towards a brighter future. Over this time, my perception of whom I am and what I call myself has changed. The first time I was brought to notice I was brown, was while living as a child for two years in Mexico. My dad (Jan Carew) had said we would move to Guadalajara, Mexico (known for artisans) or Crete. He decided on Mexico for many reasons, but explained to me that he wanted me to experience what it was like to be among the majority, to look around and see all shades of brown people doing all roles in society. From that point on, I accepted that brown was a good shade to be.

By the time I moved abroad to Sweden twenty years later, I had been working in diplomatic affairs in Washington, D.C. for two years. But I wanted to be on the outside looking in, so I applied and was accepted to several universities in England and Sweden. Considering that life was short and I would probably never get the chance again, I opted for Sweden, and spent a year and a half as an object of fascination. You don't notice color tones until everyone around you is blonde with blue eyes, and dying his or her hair black just to be different. I started dating online because I couldn't tell if those men who said you were an incredible beauty were just in lust with the difference presented by a 'Martian' or because they really saw me. That said, Swedes don't treat you any differently. They don't do hyphenated terms. You just are what you are: American, South American.

The Swedes hate war and they hated George W. Bush so much for his wars and policies that when Barack Obama was elected, they stopped the few brownies on the streets to ask if they were Americans and then offered hugs and congratulations. I remember so distinctly watching the election coverage on CNN. It was so late, and I was sitting with two Americans, a Swiss, and a Swede. We were screaming, hungover, sick from junk food, but also high on change as we watched the mass of people celebrating the moment. We had class two hours after the election results came through. On the way, a newspaper man on the street handed me the cover of the paper: it had nine faces blending into one. It started with George W. Bush and became Barack Obama. They wanted to display the visual shift in the face of American politics, but I felt it on a deeper level. The face of Americans abroad had also changed with that election. Swedes hugged us in the street, on the trains, and at the university. America was back and it was the first time I said in years without being asked, "I am an American."

Anti-climatically in Vienna, Austria, there is such diversity of people I blended right in, I spoke German and thus I was invisible. Fluidity of language is like a cloak in continental Europe. It transcends time and place. In Austria they were astounded that an American spoke German so well; no one ever asked what kind of American I was. And interestingly I stopped differentiating myself, and I finally accepted in Austria that I was an American. It felt almost naughty to not clarify, and then I had this Black Power moment where I thought, "Why does it make me deceitful to not explain all my tenths and quarters of heritage? I am an American and I shouldn't have to say black American, or African American. The brown is obvious, but my nationality is what speaks out here."

In London, your accent distinguishes you as different, not your face. People were charmed with my Midwestern vowels, more interested in where I went to university and graduate school than where I came from ethnically. I remember being put off by a comment by one of my favorite English actors, John Cleese (of *Faulty Towers*), who was paraphrased as saying that when he walks down the High Street now he doesn't know where he is: "There are hardly any English people!" That hit hard for some time, and comments sent back to him were ungracious, reminding him that England looks very much like the empire it once controlled: white, Asian, African, Caribbean. And now there are the increased numbers of Eastern Europeans. The London Olympic Committee made a big stink about how it had pitched to have the Olympics in London so as to increase jobs for Brits after the recession, only to discover most jobs had gone to Eastern Europeans. When they were asked to explain, the hiring committees said that the English hadn't applied for most of the lower wage positions because they felt they were above it. And, in addition, the Eastern Europeans were better workers, took fewer breaks, were more appreciative, and had far more qualifications. The world had changed yet again, and England was in many ways looking to America to understand how to modernize her approach to "difference", even when color was not a factor.

The starkest change in my perceptions and vice versa has come from my time in Asia, particularly my one year in Beijing, China (2002–2003) and living in Singapore since 2013. In China, people always wanted to touch me, especially the elderly. I was a 'Waiguo' (foreigner), but not anything like the categories they had in their minds. Americans were white bullies (mind you this was during the Iraq War). And for the Asian American students, the adjustment was hardest because their limited skills in Chinese meant they were often made fun of. "You're Asian, your grandparents are from Taiwan/Hong Kong/Mainland China, but you can't read or speak your own language??!!" One guy retorted, "This isn't my language anymore. Hasn't been in sixty years. Learn English," and stormed off.

I was the only black person in the IES Abroad in China program that whole year, and in that year, I saw exactly nineteen people I would classify as black. One ran up to me, a girl from Boston as it turns out, and said, "Oh my God, you're actually brown! Please tell me you speak English? I feel like a Martian who's just found another. TALK TO ME!" I don't remember ever being in a place where ethnicity was so distinguishing, so fascinating to everyone else, as in China. They wanted to touch your curly hair, touch your skin, they wanted to really understand what being different was in the most basic of senses. They played hip hop in a club and expected you to know it; they watched Baywatch reruns and said blonde All-American girls were babes and left the comment hanging. You got the message: you were a bit of an entertainment, not an object of beauty; and you had to remind yourself that outside of this bubble you were doing alright.

Now living in Singapore with a stronger handle on Mandarin, Chinese ten years later, I represent an entirely unique entity here as well. Again, there are hardly any brown people—not even Latinos or Africans. I've seen a couple of tourists and diplomats, but this is not a place of brown diversity. I run the business side of a premier fine art school for juniors (Little Artists Art Studio) and was going to the front office to collect a parent for a tour when this French Canadian white woman grasped my hand and said, "Finally, someone from home! Don't you miss seeing all types of us—white, black and Asian? I feel like I'm in another world where no one speaks French and no one seems to mind that a third of the world is totally unrepresented here!" She said it, not me; but the "us" included color variation! It was a revelation for me.

I go to the local markets or a church or a business meeting with local Singaporeans and they always want to know where I am from. If you say America they say, "Ahh, nice. My son/daughter/friend/cousin lives in Chicago, too. Great place, went on vacation there…" The women attempt to offer tips. "You're a pretty girl. Make sure you use an umbrella when you go outside and put on sun block. You're still pretty; not to worry, but you're getting dark. We have creams to treat that, you know." Indeed, there are whitening creams everywhere; and by brands with which we do not associate this type of thing in the United States: Nivea, Dove, and so on. To be dark is taboo. It means you are poor, an Indian from a lower caste.

Living in Asia and being black, you again lose the hyphen. Everyone is concerned with your skin color, yes, but more so about how it affects the look of theirs. Asians have been told for centuries that they are yellow, that this is a lesser shade than white, and they have tried to "fix" it by limiting their sun and globing on endless skin whitening creams. As my husband said, "Why would you come to the tropics and not enjoy the sun? Madness…" But it's deeper than that, and I can see it. I've seen so many variations of it, from people's happiness to discover our advancements: that slavery ended long ago in the United States; that Black Americans move freely around the world; that we speak lots of languages; that we are comfortable being varying shades of dark. But I feel like a black pioneer in Singapore. I'm co-ruling this last bastion of white dominance—culture (fine arts, linguistics, learnedness, cross-cultural exchange). I am a controller. I am tall, and curvy, and brown. I wear my hair half the month curly, the other half straight—just because I can. I hang out in an open air market or a fancy gallery opening and I'm alright, I'm comfortable.

Anthropologists claim that by 2050, the majority of people on earth will be varying shades of brown. I have no doubt. I can see it. But now, I use my difference as a tool. It gets me in the door at higher levels than I would normally be able to reach because I am memorable. Tall, brown, American, smiles and speaks Chinese—they remember you. And with that comes a great sense of responsibility. I always have to appear polished and interesting. I might be the only brownie they interact with for a year or more. I don't want to let down the group. I was accepted as a member to the prestigious University Women's Club in Mayfair, London, and I was the only young black woman I ever saw there.

I have used it for business meetings and to have some clout after starting a new education consulting company in the UK. I always used to wonder. Did I get in because I was so different? Or because I had two master's degrees and sat next to the treasurer by accident and got a nomination on the spot due to charm? I think confidence is the gift of being black Americans abroad.

My confidence to survive and thrive abroad comes from that singular childhood experience in Mexico, where I was one of many. Skin didn't get you put forward or held back, it was just skin. Language took you forward, and intelligence and language fluidity took you to the top. I often imagine I'm being watched. I turn quickly on the train and see a whole row of people looking my way. Most turn, some continue to look, and if you smile, they smile back at you. In my opinion, black Americans abroad represent the eye of change—a visual marker of progression and survival. No one expects to see us; no one blames us for being less seen.

The legacy of slavery is still in the United States and international consciousness. Obama has allowed for a shift from slavery as the primary scope. It is now about the confluence of higher education opportunities, mixed heritage, and comfort in one's body and skin. This is the new scope through which people see America. All of us out here—Black Americans included—are further engines of change, and the world is watching with bated breath to see what we achieve next.

Section 2.
FROM HERE

Buzz Palmer testifying before the U.S. Senate Committee on Southern Africa on behalf of the late senator from Illinois, Paul Simon.

WASHINGTON, D.C.

Richard Rubenstein

Richard Rubenstein is professor of conflict resolution at George Mason University. He was recently awarded an honorary doctorate by the University of Malta. Rubenstein is a Harvard trained lawyer, who earlier served as assistant director of the Adlai Stevenson Institute in Chicago, associate professor of political science at Roosevelt University in Chicago, and academic dean at Antioch Law School in Washington, D.C.

Mr. Rubenstein, an active supporter of social and racial justice causes, is a prolific author. Among his

notable works are Rebels in Eden: Mass Political Violence in the United States (1970); Alchemy of Revolution (1986); When Jesus Became God: The Struggle to Define Christianity in the Last Days of Rome (1999); and Aristotle's Children: How Christians, Muslims, and Jews Rediscovered Ancient Wisdom and Illuminated the Middle Ages (2003).

The World was Turning Upside Down

When I first met Edward "Buzz" Palmer, the world was turning upside down and Chicago, where we both lived, seemed the very fulcrum of change. I arrived in Hyde Park on Chicago's South Side in the summer of 1967 to work at the Adlai Stevenson Institute for International Affairs, a left-liberal think-tank housed at the University of Chicago. The city was hot that summer, but Detroit and Newark were hotter. In six days of rioting in Detroit, 43 people were killed, almost all of them residents of the black community; 1800 were injured; and 2000 buildings were destroyed by fire. In Newark, 26 people died, 800 were injured, and property damage was estimated at around $100 million in current dollars. It seemed pretty clear that Chicago, which had already had a "minor" riot two years earlier, and which was ruled by Mayor Richard J. Daley as his own plantation, could explode at any moment.

That was the existing situation when a black policeman named Edward Palmer, known throughout the city as "Buzz," came to the Stevenson Institute to talk to us about the situation in the city and the causes of political violence. Buzz and I were both at crossroads in our careers. I had quit practicing law and had come to Chicago to help direct the institute and see if I could write a book about violence in America. Buzz had been a Chicago patrolman since returning from his service in the U.S. Air Force and was becoming a major figure in the city's remarkable leadership cadre of radical thinkers and activists. He was already doing the organizational work that would soon produce the Afro-American Patrolmen's League, the nation's first police organization to make protection of the community against police violence one of its major goals.

That first meeting at Robie House (the Stevenson Institute's Frank Lloyd Wright-built office) was an eye-opener. Buzz was not a glib, academically polished speaker, but those who expected to hear only the wisdom of the street quickly found their stereotypes shattered. He flatly refused to frame the conflict burning up cities around the country simply as a battle between the police and the black community or a problem in "community relations." Rather, he saw it as an aspect of a much larger and more complex struggle involving overlapping, inter-related issues of race and social class and calling into question the basic structures of American society. Yes, Buzz could tell us things about police culture that only a cop would know. But his vision was society-wide. Even more, it was global, since he saw U.S. struggles as linked to conflicts taking place in other nations, both in Europe and the Third World.

In fact, although I was basically in training to be a public intellectual, Buzz was way ahead of me. A short time after that first meeting, while I was writing an article on Chicago's deteriorating race relations for The New Republic magazine, he advised me to read a book by a writer I had never heard of – a Detroit auto worker named James Boggs. I did so and was bowled over by the work of that brilliant and thorny theorist, the leader of the Detroit Revolutionary Union Movement (DRUM) and husband of the philosopher, Grace Lee Boggs. That book convinced me how little I knew about the intersection of race and class. Reading it inspired me to develop what became a lifelong interest in Marxist and neo-Marxist social theory and practice.

Not long after this, Buzz introduced me to a woman who, he somewhat grudgingly admitted, was his equal in every way: Alice Robinson Palmer, then dean of Black Students at Northwestern University. He was right; Alice was every bit as smart, tough, and imaginative as Buzz, and a better writer, to boot! Their home soon became my home away from home, and a friendship began that saw the three of us living through a blaze of dramatic events and changes, from the 1968 racial uprisings and the Democratic Convention "police riot" through the assassination of Black Panther leaders Fred Hampton and Mark Clark in 1969, the massacres at Attica Prison, Kent State and Jackson State universities the following year, and on into the years when Buzz would become the leader of COMPRAND, Chicago's most powerful voice for decent medical services for poor people and people of color, while Alice began her path-breaking career as an Illinois state senator and leader of a unique coalition of African Americans, Latinos, and white workers on Chicago's far south side.

It would take a lengthy essay to describe the projects that the three of us worked on together in subsequent years, from conferences, workshops, and political events in Chicago and Washington, D.C. to meetings at the United Nations, the European Parliament, and scores of government offices and private foundations. But I would rather tell a more personal story, since it is hard to exaggerate the impact that these two beloved friends and intrepid political warriors had on my life as a thinker and activist.

In 1969, after finishing my first book (*Rebels in Eden: Mass Political Violence* in the United States), I decided that I wanted to try college teaching. Not only did I have a feeling that this might be my true calling, but I was also becoming uncomfortable in my role at the Stevenson Institute, where my colleagues and I were coming increasingly into conflict with Edward P. Levi, president of the University of Chicago, soon to become President Richard Nixon's solicitor general. Buzz informed me that he would try to find a part-time teaching position for me at the newly renamed Malcolm X Community College, part of the Chicago City College system where Alice had also taught, and that winter, I began teaching a course on racism in America in a building on the west side of Chicago.

My start there was a bit rocky. I walked into a classroom packed with students, all African Americans, and was introduced to the class by Dr. Charles G. Hurst, the college president, who had recruited students for the college by soliciting parents door-to-door on the south and west sides. "I promised you a course on white racism in America," he told the students, "and I have found a really talented white racist to teach it!" When the applause and laughter had died down, I started talking, and by the time the class ended with a more-than-lively discussion, I realized that I was exactly where I wanted to be, where I was needed, and where I could do what I did best.

The following year, after students occupied the University of Chicago administration building, Edward Levi (the only major college president to expel student demonstrators from his university) forced me to resign from the Stevenson Institute. Now, with a wife and two small children to support, a teaching job was a necessity. The well-known African American political scientist, Charles V. Hamilton, had announced that he was leaving Chicago's Roosevelt University to become professor of government at Columbia University in New York. So, despite the fact that Hamilton was a famous scholar and the author (with Stokely Carmichael) of the manifesto, Black Power, and that I had only a JD degree and one book to my credit, Buzz and Alice teamed up with other black intellectuals to convince the Roosevelt administration to give me my first full-time college teaching job. Forty-eight years later, still teaching, writing, and agitating, I know exactly whom to thank for my first real break.

Telling this story is not only a matter of expressing gratitude to Buzz and Alice; it symbolizes a complex relationship in which all three of us have functioned as teachers and students, benefactors and recipients, and, above all, as comrades and friends. When Buzz decided to get a graduate degree, I was able to act as his professor in courses at Roosevelt University and the University Without Walls. Soon, in addition to founding COMPRAND and the Black Press Institute, he became a major player at the University of Illinois at Chicago and a senior fellow at its Institute of Government and Public Affairs. Although I had left town to teach in Washington, I often came back to participate in activities that he organized at UIC, just as he came to D.C. to participate in activities at George Mason University's School for Conflict Analysis and Resolution, where I still teach and where he served as a distinguished senior fellow.

Meanwhile, Alice was becoming one of the best known African American legislators in the country. What a pleasure it was to talk with her about her revolutionary brand of urban politics and other common interests, including the future of public higher education! During the eighties and nineties, while she and Buzz helped Harold Washington to become the first black mayor of Chicago, the three of us organized and participated in conferences in Chicago, Washington, New York, and Brussels on how to improve news media coverage of violent conflicts. And when the Palmers became co-directors of the People Programme International and began studying how to mobilize international responses to racism and xenophobia, I was an eager participant in these activities.

What role did race play in this 50-year long friendship and collaboration? The answer is paradoxical: very important in some ways, in other ways, quite irrelevant. On the one hand, Buzz's and Alice's conscious commitments to the black community played a very important role in my own personal and political development, since before I met them, like most white boys from upper-middle class suburbs, I had no intimate black friends. Getting to know them and their children introduced me to lives that were like mine in many ways, but also shaped by an experience that was definitely not mine. My Jewish background provided us with some common terms of reference, but there is simply no parallel to being black in America.

Moreover, Buzz and Alice, both incomparable networkers, opened the door for me to a whole multi-racial society. Through them I met a richly diversified group of black and white journalists, community organizers, scholars, professionals, trade unionists, political figures, and other activists who became my community—my "ethnic group" in a city divided by ethnicity. These were names and characters to conjure with in Chicago, from Kermit Coleman to Studs Terkel, Heather Booth to Otto Pikaza, Quentin Young to St. Clair Drake, and from Dick Newhouse to Harold Washington. I think of them often.

In a country like the United States, race differences never become irrelevant. Still, where the Palmers and I are concerned, they often seem beside the point, since we are joined by such strong bonds of love and shared experience, appreciation for each other's individuality, and commitment to the ultimate victory of the knechte over the herren. We have grown old together, but as Buzz and Alice always remind me, "The struggle goes on." Earlier this year, Buzz and I organized a conference at United Nations headquarters on Poverty, Inequality, and Global Conflict. Later, I consulted with Alice on activities related to the U.S. presidential election of 2016. There seems to be no end this side of eternity either to our friendship or our joint work.

Perhaps the most striking feature of Buzz's and Alice's evolution as policy-relevant thinkers and activists, however, is the movement of mind and spirit summed up in the title of this essay: "From Chicago to the World." Upon meeting the Palmers, I noticed immediately that, despite their rootedness in Chicago culture and politics, there was nothing provincial about them. They understood that they were citizens of the world, not just of one city or nation. These internationalist impulses flowered over time. I recall a series of events representative of this florescence:

-- Alice heading up the Chicago Committee in Solidarity With Southern Africa in the 1980s, and Buzz committing civil disobedience at the South African embassy in Washington, D.C. on behalf of the anti-apartheid movement

- Buzz chairing the Chicago Sister Cities program under Harold Washington and "twinning" Chicago with cities East and West
- Alice organizing the Trans-Atlantic Conference on Racism and Xenophobia with help from Buzz and financing from the Ford Foundation
- Buzz bringing delegations of African American politicians and journalists to meet with Kofi Annan at the UN with help from Alice and other friends
- My traveling to Europe and spending time in Paris, London, Brussels, Berlin, and Malta with members of Buzz's and Alice's "network" of international friends and associates, some of whom have written essays for this book.

These events and experiences made it clear that at some point—I'm not sure exactly when—the Palmers had been recognized in Europe, at the United Nations, and around the globe as unofficial ambassadors from the African American community to the world. They had become internationalists in the truest sense of the word: not by abandoning their identities as Chicagoans, Americans, people of color, or workers in order to affirm a more inclusive identity, but by affirming all these identities and not stopping until they had embraced what Marx called "species identity." For Buzz and Alice, this active membership in the global community is not just a matter of sentiment or ideology. It is based on the conviction that just as our social problems turn out in the end to be systemic and shared, the solutions also have to be arrived at collectively and globally.

An adventuresome journey, indeed! I am glad to have been along for at least part of the ride. The struggle does go on.

2. Joy Gleason Carew, PhD

Joy Gleason Carew, PhD, is the author of Blacks, Reds, and Russians: Sojourners in Search of the Soviet Promise (Rutgers University Press, 2008, 2010). She is the resident linguist and an associate professor in the Department of Pan-African Studies at the University of Louisville. She has been teaching in academe for over forty years, in institutions as varied as community colleges, major research universities, small liberal arts colleges, and historically black universities. Having designed and led numerous study abroad programs for her students and professionals from various backgrounds, she remains committed to the power of people-to-people diplomacy.

See the World Black Student, for it Surely Sees You

In 1993, when I published my article, "For Minority Students, Study Abroad Can Be Inspiring and Liberating" in the Chronicle of Higher Education, I had been teaching in higher education for nearly twenty years. It is now the close of 2015, almost twenty years after that. At that point, I was reflecting on the amazing experiences of some of my earliest programs in taking Black and other minority students abroad. Both of the student groups I described had come from Chicago community colleges—one to the USSR in 1972 and the second in 1989 to Denmark. Since then, I have worked with African American students and other first-generation college students in institutions as varied as Historically Black Colleges and Universities (HBCUs), major research universities, small liberal arts colleges, and large urban universities. And, over and over again, I have had students return with stories of how their expectations were nowhere near their actual experiences, particularly in those cases of a semester or year spent abroad. The most successful were those with whom I had worked so as to prepare them for this experience, and not just been given a ticket and told "Bye-bye." These were not always soft-focus, Disney-type stories, but inevitably stories of amazement at the ability to face the 'unknown' challenges of language and cultural difference, which then translated into new levels of self-assurance when returning home.

Which brings me to the other side of my persona. As a linguist, I have always been passionate not only about languages, but about the intersections of language and identity in general. As human beings, we all have the innate capacity to learn and use language, but also, as social beings (those animals that naturally live in social groups or packs), the ways in which these languages evolve and are used are closely tied to our identities. To live in social groups, one is constantly in negotiation and adjustment so that the communication (and survival) can work. These identities, in turn, are shaped not only by ourselves and our caregivers as we are first coming up, but also by the very powerful social cues coming at us from others—in other words, how others perceive us. For African Americans, W.E.B. Du Bois named this particular conundrum so aptly, when he coined the phrase "double consciousness." African Americans are often caught "betwixt and between"— Januses astride the worlds of "one's place" as determined by others and one's ambitions.

I came from a family that took international travel as a given. Though both parents had grown up in the segregated U.S. South, they were determined that those painful experiences and memories would not hold them or their daughter back now that they lived in Chicago. Traveling to various countries around the world, they were fully familiar with being the only African Americans in the groups or when visiting certain sites.

Could it have been their strikingly positive experiences in the USSR in 1959 that would end up inspiring me to take Russian in high school in the 1960s? It was certainly their tales and those collected from other African Americans as well as those from Afro-Russians—descendants of African Americans who had gone to the USSR in the 1920s and 1930s—that inspired the research for my book, *Blacks, Reds, and Russians,* many years later.

Our daughter, Shantoba Carew-Edwin, who now lives in Singapore, grew up in a household where travel was as natural as breathing. Her late father was the Caribbean writer, Jan Carew, who lived in many parts of the world over his ninety-two years. Growing up in the inter-war years, there was never any doubt that he would have to face challenges and prove himself in each new setting, but there was never any doubt that he should still try it.

Thus, as Shantoba observed us moving and living in different countries, sometimes where English was not the native language, this did not seem so daunting. Many years later, as a college student living in Beijing (Peoples' Republic of China) or doing graduate study in Gothenburg, Sweden, or her museum studies internship in Vienna, Austria, or now living in Singapore, she, too faced the challenges and adjusted as needed. Needless to say, her Mandarin and German skills improved dramatically as well.

As we did for Shantoba, my parents encouraged me to take foreign languages. I took Russian and French in high school and throughout my many university degrees, and I studied abroad in the USSR and France as a college student. Once I became a teacher myself, I wanted to bring this world of opportunity to my students, whether in my languages courses or otherwise, because I knew that these experiences could dramatically change their lives. It could also help educate that larger global community about African Americans.

Most of my students had never travelled outside of the United States and, equally fascinating was the fact that many of those I was encountering abroad had an equally narrow experience with Africa America. I was on the sending end of the 1989 Urban Renewal and Energy Technology (URET) program in Denmark that Peter Plenge describes in his reflection for this collection. Though I was only involved in the development of the project and the first year of the exchange, I was pleased to learn from President Homer Franklin that the program continued for several years afterwards. This speaks not only to the value of such cross-cultural exposure to the specific students, but also to the importance of such a program to the institutions sending and hosting them.

We all have the capacity to be ambassadors and to foster a grassroots peoples' diplomacy, and after our personal experiences, the opportunity to share that by word of mouth with others in our respective communities. I know that several months after Jan and I spent an extended time in African-descendant maroon villages in Suriname, that the name Joy began appearing with the birth of new girl children in those same villages. No doubt, stories about our time there with them would be shared with those children as well.

Certainly, I for almost a half a century, and Shantoba, for the last fifteen years, have frequently found ourselves disabusing persons in that larger global community by saying, "Yes, I am an African American," while watching the incredulous look on those faces. Shantoba was doing a graduate program in international museum studies at the University of Gothenburg towards the end of the George W. Bush administration and tensions were high around the fighting in the Middle East. At the time, she found that announcing oneself as an American was not always so well-received. But, when Barack Obama, the first African American presidential candidate, was elected in November 2008, everyone wanted to talk to her about this new president and the potential of the new path.

For many outside the United States, the African American exists in a narrow sphere of personas: anti-social thug or criminal, athlete or musical artist, thanks to the frequent replication of these images in the media. The fact that Shantoba could and was studying in Sweden was itself a revelation for many, who kept rechecking— "Did you say 'American' or 'African American'?" or "You're Black?", or some close version of this—when observing her brown face and self-assurance. Invariably (as they have done with me), they name a wide range of other places for her ancestry. But, that is just the point: when we, African Americans, go out into this larger world, we help people see us in our great diversity. They see us face the challenges of language and cultural difference and develop a greater appreciation for African America in general.

CHICAGO

1. Loren Taylor

Chicago-born artist Loren Taylor has a rich, diverse background, combining creative energy with community activism. His parents' involvement in civil rights and black politics in the sixties and seventies provided the foundation for Taylor's own activism, on a variety of platforms—from Occupy Chicago, to voter registration, to the Community Peace Surge to rehabbing abandoned homes for habitation for homeless families.

As a writer and journalist, he contributed a weekly column to the Chicago Defender, one of the nation's oldest African American newspapers. Taylor has lived and traveled in Europe for more than twenty years as a singer-songwriter, recording artist, instrumentalist, record producer, studio engineer and promoter. He has appeared live onstage and on television as frontman for his own projects and with well-known international recording artists. Taylor credits his unique insight into the depth of European knowledge about the African American experience to his contact with a range of Europeans, across different cultures and social strata.

Interview by David Robinson in person

There is No Place on Earth that Black Music Hasn't Reached—I Know, 'Cause I Been There

David: This is David Robinson interviewing for The World is Watching Book Project. It's November 13th Friday 2015. We're going to get started right now. Please state your full name and spelling for me.

Loren: Full name, Loren Taylor. First name spelled like Sophia Loren. L as in Lane, O-R as in Ronnie, N as in, N as in Nancy, last name Taylor; common spelling, T-A-Y-L-O-R.

David: Excellent! Loren listen up, most of the folks that we're interviewing are not US citizens. In your case, you are a US citizen that has lived abroad, worked abroad and are back. First, if you can give me a short bio; tell me about your school, tell me about growing up a little bit and tell me about what took you overseas.

Loren: Actually that's interesting. I didn't know that most of your people were going to be, you could say folks living overseas. I didn't know how many expats you were going to talk to. I guess I could start from there and work backwards, because one of the preambles I was going to share with you is I think in general any African American I think that goes to live overseas is probably just not the 'typical' expat first off.

David: I definitely agree, right.

Loren: Even in that short range, I would consider my particular you could say experience, the thing about me over there would be a bit atypical.

David: We like atypical.

Loren: The vast majority of the African Americans at least that I encountered when I was over in Europe usually get over there due to service. They generally tend to be concentrated where, of course, the U.S. military was. You're talking primarily Germany and France and a bit Italy. I wasn't in service and also too in that the fact that they get over there with service usually means wherever it is they start out is like they didn't choose it, they get assigned some place and then they kind of end up there.

Loren: My experience from right off was atypical in that sense in that I was a musician. I chose to go over there. I chose when I was going to go and I chose where I went.

David: Good.

Loren: That's the first thing that makes my experience different.

David: We find that even more intriguing, because you made choices based on what was comfortable for your own circumstances rather than being in a place like a military person and then figuring how to navigate, based on where you were located from the authorities. You made choices.

Loren: Exactly. That's the first distinction. The second thing—and I mean this is not like a qualifier, because to me it's important to the context of I think what you're trying to reach with the book—I came back for good around 2011.

David: How long did you stay over there?

Loren: About twenty years. Actually, I really lived most of my adult life over there, if you could say that; which I think definitely that also demonstrates my character without a doubt.

David: Sure, and we'll get into that too.

Loren: But in any case, like I said, I left in 2011. Why that's significant is because I was there when the first African American president was elected; but before he was reelected and before a lot of this dynamic, what's going on now particularly around—you could say—history like Black Lives Matter. I came back before we had to go through the reelection of Barack Obama, which I think in itself is kind of a turning point, before the Occupy [Wall Street] movement, the whole 99 Percent, one Percent thing and before Ferguson.

David: Got it. All key.

Loren: All very key, so it would be very interesting to hear the experience of an expat who was over there through all of that stuff, you know what I mean?

David: You will, because we have two or three that are still there.

Loren: I think those two things are very, say, key qualifiers to any perspective I give.

David: Fair enough.

Loren: I think those two things have got to be included.

David: We'll make sure we include those axial moments, those transitional moments.

Loren: Right, not in the service and got back before the shit really hit the fan. That's what you can say. That's how you capitalize it. Okay outside of that, then we can proceed.

David: Understood, very good. No, I think those are outstanding touch points as far as serving as a frame viewpoint with which to understand your experience, so that's good. All right, question; tell me first about your background. Okay, you grew up in Chicago right?

Loren: Once again it might even be useful, like you said, to somehow start at the end point and go backwards. If I talk about going over there, you could say for the first time with the intention to live there let's say in 1990. Doing that with a group of other musicians from Chicago, so the back story that you can say well got me to that point, you could say yes Chicago was not really, especially back then there were of course artists, musicians to come from Chicago, but it wasn't quite the thing even like it is now.

David: Let me interrupt you. Your musical thrust, the musical concentration, I remember starting with R&B. I remember as a kid, you playing in the basement of your parent's place.

Loren: Well, see this is why I have started at the end and going backwards, because like I said, the things was at that time, it wasn't even in the sense like it is now. Any musician that was really serious, basically eventually you think about leaving from Chicago, so this is 1990. You could say yes I've been growing up the whole time in and out of doing music and I guess by 1990, you could say I was quite some years from you could say having diverted my career path from journalism, because I graduated from Northwestern in '81 and it was like back and forth from then music after having graduated from Metro High School in 1977 after having got kicked out of lab school a few years before that. My parents hate when I say that.

To go even back through the story again I even remember like I said I'm talking about making this transition from journalism to music right? The turning point in that was the Harold Washington campaign believe it or not. I had been working in television in Rockford and Peoria, got back once again, got back to Chicago. It didn't quite work out the way I wanted to in Rockford in terms of...now how do you say it? Looking back, if you wouldn't want to think of it in that context. It's really hard to imagine just how fucking racist it was back then. I mean seriously when you think back on this stuff, sometimes you take it really for granted because it's kind of what we lived through and survived it.

David: We were armored up. We knew.

Loren: We knew it, so we survived and didn't make a big deal out of it, but when you think back on it now, it's like, "Fuck, it was racist as hell." Okay it didn't work in Rockford, I come back in Chicago. I was working at City News Bureau which most folks don't know it...City News Bureau is like [a] local version of Associated Press or UPI or one of these wire services. What they do is they have the staff and a lot of the, at that time especially, news sources used it, because then they cut out the redundancy. We had at least all the radio stations, but also newspapers were the clients.

David: Wouldn't you say it was also one of the legendary training grounds where you cut your teeth to be a real reporter?

Loren: Right and that was the thing. It's like, okay even after … having worked in TV, yes City News Bureau was just like, "Somebody got shot, go cover it."

David: Go be there.

Loren: This was during the Harold Washington campaign. They always made sure that they had just enough blacks, just enough, not more than they needed, but just enough. I somehow wound [up doing] the de facto covering [of] the Harold thing and I got to know this is when Bill Wallace was more or less his right hand guy.

David: Yes, tell me about that man.

Loren: I mean it's the whole almost where do I start thing? Do you really want me to talk about…?

David: We're going to elevate it. Give me the essence of it if you can.

Loren: Well, it was a thing that definitely got me to quit being a journalist, because it was a thing that gave me the thing of saying, "I want to participate." Once again what was really weird I mean as I think weighing between the boomers and generation X, people don't really know what this generation was about. Not much was really said about it, because you really are with a fit in both things. You were being conditioned onto shit that you know is already out of date, is already passé, but the new thing hasn't really been set yet.

David: Well said yes. I often talk to my kids about that. We came up….

Loren: They don't know. It's hard to explain what that's like.

David: …in the remnants of real, straight up in your face overt racism, we came in the last vicissitude of it.

Loren: But it was still a reality?

David: It was still there.

Loren: For instance okay, the South Shore Cultural Center which is now owned by the [Chicago] Park District used to be the South Shore Country Club. It was private and it was… no Jews and Blacks. I could watch in my bedroom window people flocking on the beach and riding horses and playing golf, but I could not walk two or three blocks to actually go over there. This is my lifetime. This is not a story from my grandpa. This is my lifetime….

my grandmother's mother was already six years old when slavery ended. It [wasn't] that long ago. It really wasn't. We're really only one generation out of apartheid and most Black families not more than two generations out of poverty. The ones that aren't poor now...

David: Are currently still suffering from that yes.

Loren: ...right okay. In light of all that and the context of what it is that we're talking about, I can say I came up in this time when all of this shit was changing and certainly it was in journalism. I'm getting my journalism going at a time when the standard model was they were training, before they knew it was getting ready to blow up anyway. Nobody was reading the newspapers. Do you know what I'm saying? What was going on with TV was like something new that most of our professors didn't know. When we were doing our internships, professors would come to visit and they would be like, "Wow, what is all this shit in here?" We was being taught something that they knew was already out of date. It was on the way out.

David: On a footnote from your journalism days, I remember when I was with the Detroit News. I told the old timers how to operate a word processor. That was the new thing, coyote system. I don't know if you remember that name, but that was the first one.

Loren: Now and once again you talk about you remember days gone by one of the opportunities that I had as a student, literally that technology makes it not necessary anymore. I was a copy clerk which is the modern incarnation of the copy boy, because back in the day the stuff had to be transported by hand. Basically, once again I'm in an era where they knew all of that shit was getting ready to implode on itself, but I got the benefit of it being the copy clerk who physically took the headline from the hand of the news editor and walked it down to the lithograph room and handed it to the guy. Or when the reported needed some background, they could hand me some piece of paper and I would go into the library and get an envelope of news clippings.

David: That was the morgue. We called it the morgue, going to the morgue.

Loren: Yes, that was called the morgue. That shows you how long I've been away from that shit. Yes, I went into the morgue and then they handed you something. Every now and then maybe you were looking through some microfilm for some shit that was. In general even if you found it, then you were still going to the desk and saying, "I'm going to give you this," because the guy wasn't going to get off of his fat ass and go to the morgue himself. I mean how would you say it? I didn't have much of trouble leaving that to go into music. It wasn't that difficult. I say all this preamble because I remember of course your elders and folks like that it's like, "Boy have you lost your mind?"

David: I get that because I know your parents.

Loren: "You quit a job?" Actually believe it or not, my parents especially my dad was actually cool. He was excited actually. He really lived, which most folks of my family would have known; he lived vicariously through all this shit. He was like the number one guy.

David: That's cool, that was encouraging you to just go for it.

Loren: Well, he was into this kind of thing like he really did believe the whole life is short thing. He really held to that. Prestige-wise, it would be cool to have the son was the journalist, but he got over it, to put it that way. Of course, folks the aunts and uncles it was, "Are you crazy?"

David: "Are you crazy? You could do a really good job."

Loren: Well, how do you leave a job when you ain't got a job? That's that generation.

David: Definitely that generation yes.

Loren: Why would you quit? Why would you leave a job unless you already have another job? Well, because I find it to be much more fulfilling. Now let me tell you what one of my uncles said. I say this is the classic one was my father's brother. Well, I find I wanted to do something I think is more fulfilling for me. He says, "Well, let me tell you Loren, your problem is that you confuse about what a job is." "Okay, run it down." He says, "You're not supposed to like your job."

David: That's old school. That's how old school is like.

Loren: He says, "Your job is a means to an end. A job is what you do to take care of your family. It provided you some net worth. You've got your ass backwards kid."

David: Right, so it's not about enjoying what you do?

Loren: Right. "Who said you have to like it? You already screwed so we don't even have to continue this conversation. You already screwed up. Whatever decision you made after that, it's got to be the wrong one, because you're starting off wrong."

David: Your premise, your theorem is wrong.

Loren: You aren't supposed to like your job. Anyway I decided to like my job and I decided that I didn't like the United States either, because this is also a good time to question all of that shit, because since I wasn't going to…what I told people is you see the thing is, I didn't even really realize it till I got out. Now I fast forward it to 1990 and it was like they all wave and like, "Don't come back too soon."

It was even known from how talking to guys, the way that you do it was like in a sense or form of being the illegal alien. That was the intention from the get. It was like that which is strange, but Americans we knew we'd get away with it, so you buy the ticket, the round trip because it's cheaper and you ain't coming back.

David: That's interesting.

Loren: The idea is that you try to stay there as long as you can and you only come back really when you've got to, because there's no work.

David: Did you have any contacts?

Loren: Yes. That was the one of the thing I remember. Once again, you tell the truth, the way it's really told. The jazz thing, the circle was probably the only interracial and multicultural thing I'd seen in Chicago. At the time there were quite a few of them like jazz clubs down north Division [Street] and around the area.

David: Pools and all that.

Loren: All that stuff, and so I was part of this little network. There was one guy I remember was a piano player and somehow you met someone who was going back and forth from there and like, "Guys you've got to come over, you've got to come over, you've got to come over," Scandinavia… because nobody had heard of it. We'd heard of London and Paris, but why would we go to Scandinavia? Of course he came back one thing he said, yes he had a photo scrapbook.

David: Beautiful landscapes.

Loren: Well, I mean listen, because see that was the thing. We're even going back here. The thing that pulled me away or even made it that music was the thing for me in the first place since I have a cousin. He's a bit older than me who is actually kind of an anomaly too, because as a teenager he got in with more or less the part-time crew. This was when Curtis Mayfield was ramping that whole thing up. He played on a ton of...

David: I remember that. I remember meeting him.

Loren: Yes, right. He played on a ton. They thought it was cool, because I was like smarter in the whole lab school thing. As a kid I was smart enough. I could sit around adults. I knew how to act around adults. They thought it was cool for me, literally man I'm like eleven, twelve backstage at shows with these guys with their groupies smoking fucking blunts as long as... your arms and I'm just sitting there. Literally, after a while, it was like I wasn't there.

David: Exactly, you're the kid, almost famous...

Loren: I wasn't even there. I saw a lot of that shit which was one of the reasons I left and my mom, of course, is definitely afraid of me following that, because certainly at the time too, that was the immediate association: musicians and drugs...

David: And at the time, too.

Loren: Like I said, it turned out I was the only one. This is the very long answer to your question if I had a contact there. The piano friend of ours that was a piano player, he was already there in Oslo, Norway and we were going to go meet him there. Of course in the end, I was the only one that went. I remember that. I said, "Man look. I don't give a f--- what you've got to say about it, at least your ass is going to be at the airport when I get there." I demanded, "If you even just say, 'Okay, cool to see you,'" I want to see one person I know." I kind of demanded that he be there and meet me. We worked together for about like six months or so.

David: What's your instrument?

Loren: I play five different instruments. I was the studio recording engineer.

David: I remember you with a trumpet.

Loren: For instance, I got paid to do that. I toured with, do you remember Rufus Thomas' "[Do The] Funky Chicken"?

David: Sure, yes the whole Stax Records crew.

Loren: Right. I toured with him in Europe. Also a guy named Eddie Floyd. Actually, somehow that was one of the contacts I had when we got that was booking these old R&B guys and it's almost nostalgia for Europeans.

David: Now Rufus Thomas had a wife, they were really tight in terms of the music. Is that right? Was she with him?

Loren: Yes, but I mean no. Basically, like I said, he was still literally at age seventy touring, doing tours in Europe.

David: "Funky Chicken" and all of that?

Loren: Basically, there was only like three or four songs that he was really known for over there, but between all that…it was enough for him to haul together a 70-minute show or something of those three songs and some other blues [songs], because he's known for that. That's the thing that people don't know about Rufus, what made him different than a lot, a lot, a lot of those other guys from that era of Stax or any of the folks in that R&B era is that he wrote a lot of those songs. He still had a lot of the rights on those songs.

Loren: He wrote for a lot of people, too, and people covered a lot of his [songs] too. "Walking the Dog," I think it was like …about three hundred different registered recordings of that song. These are the kind of experiences that I had that gave me, you could say, a different perspective of in a sense you could say what it means to be a Black Americans. Like for instance, it was very clear to see how Black culture was also a commodity.

David: Tell me about that.

Loren: Well…African Americans really knew how they were regarded in the rest of the world; a lot of the pathological self-hatred type behavior you see just literally wouldn't exist.

David: Give me an example. In your experience, a couple of examples.

Loren: Okay, the first example would be the very tangible one. I say that Black culture, if it was conceived correctly, for us it would be the same resource like the oil is for the Arab countries. That's how much in demand it is.

David: Fascinating; it's that valuable.

Loren: Certainly...the largest impact is on youth. We're just suddenly this time realizing here in America, where Black America goes, young America goes.

David: Pew did a study recently which tracked all that.

Loren: That's worldwide, man. I'm [in] Thailand, seeing posters of Thai rap groups.... There literally wasn't one corner of the planet where—I mean literally—I could be in the little smallest, remotest village in Sicily in the mountains and they knew who we are. They know who we are. There's not one spot, place on the planet that does not know who we are.

David: Man, that's amazing. We'll talk about it.

Loren: To the smallest, remotest village in Africa. That's what I'm saying. If we knew that, man, like I said a lot of this pathological self-hatred behavior...

David: Well, you know that's part of what we're trying to do with this piece.

Loren: Everyone else has figured out how to capitalize off of it, electronic music, house music and dance music is the pop music in Europe. It's basically our music, just the same way that they expropriated blues and turned it into rock 'n' roll, a lot of what you would call electronic dance music. Some of it of course, now, is so far away from that; house music, roots and, yes, but that's the core of it. That's the core of it, and so they've figured out how to turn it into like really a billion dollar industry now. Fortunately, there are a handful of Black folk, and they've also been able to export it back to United States.

I should be in LA right now running a club doing that. I was like part of the thing that set the foundation for that and then walked away from it.

Loren: Okay, we know now that you can say, the digital highway, whatever it is that you want to call it, this is now the network that is going to transmit information of which we don't necessarily acknowledge it, but entertainment really is just another form of that. I'm talking about movies, music, any of that.

Entertainment by its nature is just another form of contact and in fact the new paradigm more or less just relegates all content really into one large group. Like I said, so I'm going over to Europe more or less at a time where all of this is changing. All of this is in kind of flats. I suppose I didn't know that I was going over there as much you could say for my own education as I was to try to have some sort of career goals.

The reason for going over there was this idea that okay however motivated I was by career interest, there was a core thing that wanted to have some artistic integrity to it. As I said, it was my impression that the racism in American society permeated through all levels of it. Artistically, as a Black person, you were really very limited in what your artistic expression could be.

David: Because they were setting parameters, defining it based on their business structures.

Loren: Well, also and some dirty secrets that they didn't want let on even to the people inside the thing, like the dirty secret that hip hop almost from its inception was designed for white people, fascinating. From its inception, the vast bulk of the audience for rap music has been, is and always will be white boys who...

David: Who are able to take discretionary income and spend money.

Loren: Right, okay and so every time I hear someone talk about hip hop poisoning the minds of our youth, yes right.

David: That might have been a side effect.

Loren: No, no the thing is because those kids knew that they could listen to that shit and one day they would take off the Pumas.... They always knew that.

David: Yes, they knew that. They grew up knowing that.

Loren: They always knew that and their parents that. That's why their parents didn't have a problem with them listening to that.

David: "Johnny, when will you stop listening to that stuff?"

Loren: Well, I'll give you this one. I tell this story. I remember being in Zurich and I don't know how I bumped into...a conversation with some Americans. I think they were tourists. They were all thirty-something, right. They were talking about a friend of theirs, a mutual friend of theirs. They said, "Yes, Bob still listens to hip hop. He still listens to hip hop." They all knowingly went, "Aah?" which means that they...

David: He has to jump back on the white path, on the path, yes.

Loren: ...one of them was a Black guy, but that was the thing, but he still listens to hip hop. He still listens to hip hop. The thing of it is, it's kind of the same thing over there. It's strange, the influence on the culture, how would you say it? This is the one thing I was thinking about, I don't know if you could say influence is even the word for it, because did African Americans or do African Americans influence culture in these other places? Yes. It's not so easy to try and put the finger on it per se, but it does because as I said, our presence is so wide spread and who we are is so known and familiar to folks. There has to be some effect in that way. But then, what exactly is it? I mean I don't know that.

David: As you know though, what we're developing here is the seeds for this discussion, for this thing to begin to take root in the African American scholar community and among the young hip hop cats. I want them to read what you just said or hear it and say, "Damn."

Loren: Well, I'll put it this way. They will be like you said. What you can do is you can develop even some kind of practical sides to it. I've had those kinds of visions, the whole kind of like integrated system for the entertainment from the top down.

Loren: [They] embrace all of these types of black culture, like they embrace hip hop, for example. Intuitively, they know that what these guys are talking about in their music doesn't really speak to their culture. Then what can they...identify with? Well... one they pull a part of it that they can identify with, for instance, "Fuck the police". They didn't have anything to really be pissed off at the police about, but that's kind of a rite of passage to have some kind of "fuck the police" type of thing in your life.

The other one was, all of the—for lack of a better word—let's say the support functions around the DJ culture. [That] was really intense over there. They couldn't necessarily produce music that was saying anything that really spoke anything. Most European hip hop artists, to me, they did kind of come off as being silly. They didn't mind being that kind of a comic. Like I said, there wasn't really anything in their culture that could be ...

David: You couldn't be angry about nothing.

Loren: …while they idolized all these guys, they couldn't really emulate their music. The DJ culture was really intense; the graffiti art culture was super intense, dance crews, fashion. They gravitated towards all of those kinds of things, which was boon for the marketers, a boon for the money guys. It's like this is the part of the thing that these kids can relate to. Every town that I went to in Europe had a hip hop store and that was a constant thing of the expat community trying to figure out what from over there can we bring over here. How many discussions did I get into people that wanted to open a store for the gear?

One cat that I knew that wanted to have his own label, [was] a black guy from Jamaica who grew up in Europe. He's going to get his clothes label. Of course he's black enough so he had enough white kids who wanted to [be] around him.

Loren: The reason why all of that is important, even as a preamble of anything else is like I said, culture. It's much more significant to them than it is for us because what we're looking for would be to have a guy that would be the vice president here.

David: I want to have you try this sort of experiment. You can't be black, particularly a black male in this country and feel the eyes on you when you go to Macy's or Nordstrom or in a community that you're a neighbor to them.

Loren: Unless you've spent your whole entire life living in a place where you were not like everybody else and so that doesn't register. Literally it doesn't register.

David: And maybe it doesn't register, but me and you, we know.

Loren: It kind of doesn't register with me anymore, I had to relearn that when I got back over here. I remember my dad when he came over and visited me …

David: You're on the right track though.

Loren: I'm already on it.

David: That disappeared over there, is that what I'm hearing?

Loren: Just because the thing that it is, it got to be that this was kind of like normal. I remember the first time my dad and mom came to visit. He said, "Don't you get tired of people looking at you all the fucking time?" I'm like, "No."

David: You became desensitized to it. When they look at you...

Loren: I got to be ... either proud to be the ambassador, [or] proud to show them we didn't have a tail.

David: Now was it more curiosity or was it straight up racism?

Loren: 99.8 percent of the time curiosity. I can really count on my hand the number of times that I experienced overt racism.

David: Fascinating. Twenty years?

Loren: Yes, but the racism in the society wasn't kind of like a backdrop that's part of the atmosphere; this is a whole other story. I only literally experienced... well, yes, like when I got deported.

David: Tell me about that. Where were you?

Loren: In Zurich, when I got deported. I've been deported from Europe twice. I know when they talk about illegal aliens and that whole shit and the immigration, I lived it. I lived that shit. I lived it.

David: Why did you get deported?

Loren: Both times I got deported more or less for like either extending a visa or basically being an illegal alien, one that was working illegally. First time I got thrown out of Norway, basically I got caught working illegally. They came up in the club.

David: That's the thing, how did they know? Were they watching?

Loren: In Norway somebody dropped the dime on me. There's mob everywhere you go, or some version of it. Feuding mobsters. I got caught in the middle of that bullshit. They dropped the dime on me you could say.

David: That's deep.

Loren: I was working for his asshole and then started working for this asshole, who didn't like this asshole and so this asshole dropped the dime on me. They sent the biggest guy from the precinct to walk into my gig and arrested me. They were cool about it because basically they were just like, "We just want you to pay your taxes. We know that if you work without a visa you're not going to pay. This is what you do. Here, fill these out." The drill is you can't do it from there. You have to be in your home country and do it [there].

David: Then come re-file and all that kind of thing.

Loren: I was back in maybe two to three months and I married a Norwegian.

David: Tell me about that.

Loren: She was from a small town. It was when I was in a small town, and so yes it was something like ... [it] was exotic for both of us. That wasn't my shtick to do the gangster thing; I was more the jazzy thing, more sophisticated. I fell in love. We fell in love.

David: That part I understand.

Loren: It was cool. The thing was, it was in the kind of a place, certain places that I have been, there was a kind of a racial tension that was born over a lot of the kinds of things that exist even here; competition for perceived resources, kind of entrenched groups that have vested interest in promoting a racist agenda. Certain places you wouldn't have that, there would not even be enough mass of foreigners that they would even feel threatened by it.

David: Right, there would be no reason even to organize because there's like three brothers.

Loren: Her father tried to have a little bit of a problem with it, but he even came and he said, "Look I couldn't fake it. I tried to figure out the reason why my daughter shouldn't be with a black guy, and I couldn't really find one."

David: That alone expresses a certain intelligence about this that may not even exist. My dad likes to say that Europeans, based on their longer history of dealing with all kinds of things with respect to other folks at their door steps on their borders, have a much more intelligent viewpoint about inter-relations with us. Would you agree with this?

Loren: Yes, because first of all the thing of it is, we have this impression of white people. I remember ... calling my dad. I would say, "Dad, I've figured out who white people are." He's like, "What are you smoking over there? What the hell are you talking about?" I say, "I know who white people are." When we talk about white people, we just use it as a kind of a short hand, but over there they actually have a sense of it.

David: Tell me about that.

Loren: For instance, when I was in Scandinavia, I actually was hooked up with these Italian guys. They had a band. It was like two Italian guys, a few Scandinavians were playing with them, so they found me, and then I started [to] front the band and then they really were able to work.

David: Because of you.

Loren: Right.

David: And because of that thing we talked about earlier, that thing that we bring.

Loren: It worked out for both of us, but they would tell stories about how when they first came to Scandinavia, they would hear Scandinavians saying, "You guys must be happy to be in a white country finally." These are Scandinavians talking to Italians.

David: Fascinating.

Loren: [The] Italians, definitely, they had the sense of it and they would tell you, "We've got African blood in us." They were serious about that, especially the further south you went.

Loren: When we think of white people, what our thing of white people is, is a short hand for that. What Anglo Saxon Protestant the rest of Europe knows that, too.

Loren: We think Jewish people are white. No, they ain't. They know some Europeans. I was like, [I] get it. I called my father, and he said, "What are you talking about? You know we had our own version of it." I said, "Dad, this is not the same thing." This is a whole different thing. We are like the commodity that helped them build their nation, so they love us."

Loren: I learned more about Africans living in Europe than I ever could being here. The white man didn't take us out of Africa. What the white man did was park the boat on the shore and then we went and got some of our brothers and sisters and brought them to the boat. This is like anything else. If you know what this guy is buying, you are going to sell him the good shit so when you went and raided that village you didn't take the bullshit, you took the good shit. Three-fourths of us died in the holocaust on the way over so the good shit; the strongest of the strong. What they do with this other species is that they try every generation that you don't wipe out. What happens?

David: They get stronger.

Loren: It just gets stronger.

David: It's the evolution

David: Let's talk about the future, because you've raised some fascinating points about who we really are, our community, if we really knew how amazing we really were which is the essence of this thing and the fact that everywhere around the world, they [emulate] it. What would you say to young African Americans here about your knowledge that you acquired there?

Loren: What I would say is that, if you're talking about projecting all this in the future, where can this go? As I said, we're respected in terms of this idea of resiliency, culture and also some of this idea of the creative thing. Can we now, so to speak, bump that up where we're really talking about using that, for lack of a better word, building their nations? There's a lot of ways that we can describe that, but certainly I think one of them would be to excel. There's always this question about what is it that we want? Do we want to be included in what they are doing here in Chicago Booth or do we want to have our own Chicago Booth? That's always a question.

David: We had heard that, gave it up and the whole Booker T. [Washington]-[W.E.B.]Dubois piece; the whole question of why we give up what we had in order to try to get what we think they had and we never really were able to assimilate.

Loren: This is one that I've been really thinking a lot about lately, because there's a bit of water treading going on. I think the conversation sounds a little bit staid and stale and that they want to keep talking about it in the same paradigms or framework, for lack of a better word, that it was talked about ten years or twenty, thirty years ago. It's the twenty-first century. It's been fifty years since the March [on Washington].

David: Did [the Civil Rights movement] ever come up in the course of your time there? Any discussions with them about Martin King or Malcolm or anything like that?

Loren: To be honest with you, the only one they really are familiar with is Martin. Malcolm... there might have been some people who were a little bit curious about that when Spike's movie came out; but the only figure that they are really familiar with is Martin Luther King. I think it's because he was assassinated so young and that he seems to be in a sense embodied in… that movement. It would be a very, very limited number of people that would be familiar of Malcolm X.

David: Unlike, say, Duke Ellington or Miles Davis.

Loren: Certainly, these guys would be much more well-known than Malcolm. Like I said, he becomes any of our 'cultural' heroes, even some of the ones that would be obscure here. I'm sure there are probably more Europeans that are familiar with Calloway as the most known African American or Josephine Baker.

David: Let me ask you, did you perceive or see any clear difference between the way Africans, African Africans and [African Americans were perceived]?

Loren: Yes. Yes, I always would tell people that while in Europe, I wasn't a black man. I was a Black American musician, that's one African Americans were dealt with in your experience word. I had to always remind them not to put me in a special category. Then also too what you start to find is like I say basically just all foreigners, this is the growing pain that Europe is still going through, the idea of the foreigners. They're not sold on the idea of multicultural society or that is itself a good thing. In every country you go there is a segment of Deutschland for the Deutsch.

David: When I go to Paris, I experience that in France quite a bit. France for the French, Le Pen.

Loren: That was one sentiment that was also starting to be a little bit on the rise when I left. Someone told me that this isn't the time to be going back for a while because you could see that sentiment becoming almost mainstream. I left Switzerland to go to Italy, so I think the last two, three years I was in Europe, I was in Italy.

David: Okay, last question. And this already captures all that you've said, but I'm going to bring it to a fine point here. What insights, opinions or perspectives would you give to African Americans in this uncertain era as they continue to struggle, to repel racism to maintain hard-won gains and perhaps most importantly find footage and advancement going forward?

Loren:: Build the nation around economics, but this one that is a bit…the only qualifier in this is African Americans, Americans are probably going to have to reconcile with this nation within a nation.

David: I've been talking about this just today, nation within a nation without a nation. You get that?

Loren: Yes. One of the things that my travels around the world have shown me is that there's no parallel for it. There's no model for it. There's none.

David: There's none, because unlike every other group that came over here, they're a nation within a nation that still has a nation. We don't.

Loren: If you go to these other places, one of the things that I was relieved about when I finally moved back from Europe was that they were preoccupied with nationality. One of the things that was really different about a lot of them, not everyone, but a lot of the European society, they really believe that your national identity and your ethnic identity was really the most salient fundamental [part] of your character and anything else about you was built on top of that.

This is particularly salient for the expats in any particular country. We think of the Americans, but a French guy living in Florence is also an expat, the Tamil who's living in Germany and the Eastern European who's living in Denmark is also an expat. These people are fierce about their national and ethnic identity. As a Black American it was odd because at the same time they didn't have a sense of what it meant to be an African American, because I tried to explain to them, "Yes I am an American, but dot, dot, dot. It's a whole new thing.

David: Right.

2. Chef Sara Louise Phillips

Sara Louise Phillips grew up in Pittsburgh, Pennsylvania. As a girl, Phillips imagined a career in fashion design. She also had a love of travel. An opportunity to travel the world as a flight attendant led her to apply for flight attendant training. Phillips went on to become one of the first African American flight attendants to regularly staff international flights. After a thirty-year career in flight service, Phillips had the opportunity to pursue a career in another favorite pastime: preparing good food. As a child, Phillips learned from her mother and grandmother more than just the basics of cooking; she also learned the importance of fresh ingredients and an appealing presentation. Years later, she launched Chef Sara's Café. The cozy restaurant nestled in Chicago's South Shore neighborhood offers an incomparable combination of good food with healthy ingredients, making it a popular destination for many in the community.

Flying While Black—
Breaking the International Color Barrier 30,000 Feet in the Air

David: It is November 14, 2016. This is David Robinson. I'm proceeding with the interview of Chef Sara. Just to begin, Chef Sara, for the record, please state your full name, your title or occupation and where you live.

Sara: My full name is Sara Louise Phillips. I'm in the Chicago South Shore area.

David: South Shore area, perfect. Can you tell me a little bit about what it was like growing up? Did you grow up here in a town or down south?

Sara: I grew up in Pennsylvania, Pittsburgh to be exact. I have five siblings, so there're six of us. We grew up and always had a home. I'm very proud about that because we didn't have to live in an apartment. We lived in housing there. My mother was a very strong woman about making sure that her children were able to have a profession. She taught me how to sew and which, then when I grew up I wanted to always be a seamstress. I went to school for fashion design.

David: No kidding. I didn't know that.

Sara: Yes, I did. In the midst of going to school for fashion design the airline started hiring and I let go.

David: Now, back then it was TWA, Pan Am...

Sara: American, Braniff, all the old carriers, so just about five.

David: Now, around what year are we talking about?

Sara: We're talking about 1971.

David: Okay, good. Very exciting.

Sara: I quit going to school and went to interview for that because to me that was the thing, is to be able to fly around the world.

David: Why? What was exciting? Just that you get a chance to get out in the world and see things and experience things?

Sara: Well we're going to back this a little bit as I was growing up. When I was growing up, I used to always have these dreams where I couldn't keep my feet on the ground. I'd always fly above the clouds. One day I asked my mother. I said, "Mom, why is it that in my dreams I can't keep my feet on the ground? I'm always above the clouds. Above everybody, looking down." She said, "You have great expectations." She told me that as a little girl.

Then once I used to watch all the time the girls coming in to the hotel because I had to take the bus to school and I always went through downtown Pittsburgh. I'd see the flight attendants getting off their bus going into the hotel and I say, "I would sure like to do that."

David: That's good.

Sara: When the opportunity arose, I decided you know what? I'm going for this because at that time they didn't have a lot of blacks.

David: I was going to ask you would have to have been a pioneer in that right?

Sara: Yes. Well, I think that the girls in the late sixties I think they went far back as '65 maybe '68 they were starting to hire some black women.

David: But not international though right?

Sara: No, because you had to have a language and you know, we didn't speak languages unless you were from Honduras or somewhere around in there or Panama because my roommate was from Panama. She was able to get in right away international because she spoke Spanish. Having said that, "I decided well this is what I want to do. I'm going to go on and fly." Jessie Jackson was a key member in getting us on because he had...

David: Tell me about that yes.

Sara: He had threatened the airlines to march on airlines because there were no black flight attendants. That's when the doors opened up for us . I really, really appreciate him for that because he did march. I think it was in the seventies, he had started threatening. By '71 they started opening up the doors and hiring a lot of blacks.

David: Interesting. Okay, very good. So tell me about the hiring process and what was that like?

Sara: The hiring process was a big deal because of the fact that they wanted black women that were beautiful black women. I'm not saying that I was...

David: Well, you're fine Chef Sara. You're all right. You could do this.

Sara: They told us out of every one hundred women interviewed they only took about 25 percent.

David: They told you because they had to have a certain look.

Sara: Exactly.

David: Now today they couldn't say that.

Sara: They can't say that today. I remember distinctly when I went on interviews that the way they interviewed me, I had to stand up like the sun facing me and see an image of me. She looked at me like a passenger would look at me. They made us stand in front of a window with the light shining in.

David: Really?

Sara: Because you would have the light shining in from the airplane. I didn't understand all of this, but she made us stand up tall. If I have hair on my arms and they were darker, they would make you shave your hair. They made the white girls do that, they didn't make the black girls because...

David: Yes because white girls got the little fuzzy stuff on.

Sara: Exactly. We weren't supposed to be able to wear glasses, but you had to have a certain vision and you had to be a certain height. You couldn't be below five, I think 5'5" because you had to be able to reach up into the overheads, reach up into the ovens, because everything was high. That was it.

David: Fascinating. Was it mostly ladies that were interviewing you or were there men, too?

Sara: They were mostly ladies interviewing. I never had men.

David: These were flight attendants? Like, experienced flight attendants?

Sara: Exactly, people that were already in top positions. They were in charge of the cosmetic part of it as far as keeping us [in] our makeup, our hair. We could wear afros, but they had to be trimmed afros. We couldn't wear braids, no braids. Not a lot of color in our hair. We had to have it simple. Then when I went to training, they wanted to let the white girls do our hair, but they couldn't do anything with our hair. We had to go off the premises, get our hair done, and come back and they would okay it.

David: Fascinating. Tell me what the training was like.

Sara: The training was unbelievable, because it was, like, one black to every class.

David: How big were the classrooms?

Sara: Our classes were about twenty to twenty-five people in class. We even had living learning centers. I went through TWA's training which was based in Kansas City, Overland Park in Kansas City. They had this fantastic training center that had just opened up because in the earlier days, these people were trained at a hotel. Well we were trained at the new premises, at the new base.

David: Simulated and all of that.

Sara: Everything, it was just like a college campus. We even had a cafeteria where we would go and eat. Then in between our classes it was like a living learning center where we would sit down and talk between our classes, get to know different people. Well, right away we gravitated toward each other because we were the only one in the class.

Sara: They would stand upstairs—because it was like in a round, they would stand upstairs—and watch us; our every move. Then when we got evaluated, we got evaluated at least, maybe, three or four times before we graduated. Our training was six and a half weeks, yes. I remember distinctly my trainer, my instructor, he pulled me to the side and said, "You know, Sara, I see during your breaks, you black girls sit around and talk with each other. We don't want to see that. We want you to mingle with everybody." We had to stop doing that and be with the white girls.

David: Okay, well did he say that to the white girls though?

Sara: No.

David: No, because that's normal for them. For us it's, "Oh, black people, you know."

Sara: That's right, they didn't want us to hang together like that. We could after class, but not during the session.

David: Interesting.

Sara: That was pressure.

David: Did you pick up any overt kind of racial things? Some of it sounds like they just weren't accustomed to having black people around; they just didn't know how we are.

Sara: That's it.

David: Was there any other stuff that you all had to say, "Wait up. I can't do this."

Sara: No.

David: Okay.

Sara: Like I said they pulled us in, one by one, and then we would compare it afterwards because we all lived in a dormitory, too. There was, like, four girls to a dormitory. Then it was like a big living learning center inside the dormitory. I think the dormitory had like maybe four rooms to each dormitory. They were all different names. We had an African setting, we had an Italian setting.

David: Really?

Sara: Yes, it was interesting.

David: Now, do they still train like that, do you know?

Sara: No, they don't train like that anymore. In fact, their training is cut down. It used to be six and a half weeks. The last time I checked I think they were only going five weeks because see we had so many planes to learn; we had more planes to learn. Now there's not as many planes.

David: Fascinating, because that was the era where they had introduced the jumbo jet. Concorde, I think, were starting to fly later.

Sara: Concorde was still there.

David: Then the DC-10 was pretty popular that time.

Sara: We had the L-1011.

David: L-1011.

Sara: Right and then we had the MD-80s, DC-9s, 727 stretch, 727 regulars; we had 707s. So we had a lot of airplanes to learn in five and a half weeks. The pressure was on.

David: Was it really?

Sara: The pressure was deep.

David: Tell me, what is a class like? What were you learning?

Sara: Well, our classes were set up where as we learned an airplane a week. No, we learned two or three airplanes in a week.

David: You had to learn obviously the number of seats and you know all that kind of things.

Sara: What was most important about learning the airplane was learning where the oxygen equipment was, how to open that door. It was pretty fast because all we had to do was make sure we knew where all the equipment was, how to open that particular door, how many passengers, they didn't hold it to us because they took seats in and out all the time.

Then we had to learn how many crew members that would be flying the airplane because we had a lot of two-men cockpit crew members, then we had two men. The larger the airplane got, the more men we had in the cockpit. Then the service was the biggest thing they impressed upon us.

David: Very good. Now you're trained up, and how do you get placed? How does that process go?

Sara: Well, after our training we got placed to different domiciles, you know, and that's where we flew out of. When I finished graduating there was only two I think three domiciles open; it was Chicago, New York and L.A. All of us would get together and say well, we're all going to New York but I slyly put Chicago down first. They was mad at me, I said, "Look I got family in Chicago. I'm going to Chicago first."

David: You got it good.

Sara: I didn't think Chicago would open up. Sure enough Chicago opened up I got Chicago. Everybody else went to New York.

David: Fascinating. You did domestic for a while.

Sara: I did domestic for my first, I'd say for my first ten to fifteen years flying. I flew out of Chicago domestic.

David: In that ten to fifteen years did something change where…the opportunity to travel internationally opened up? How did that happen?

Sara: I think it was 1978 [when] it opened up for us to go international. The rules started changing because they could no longer stipulate that everybody had to speak a certain language. Then we also had men as flight attendants; they came on in 1971 or 72.

David: Was there a union or anything yet?

Sara: Yes, we had a union, and our union made sure that everything would change according to how we would set up because we had men, now. We had to share rooms before and that was horrible.

David: I bet.

Sara: It was horrible because the white women felt that they shared the rooms with us, but they were treating us still real bad, you know. They'd use the towels up, they'd go out and spend the night with a guy, bring a guy home. I went through all of that.

Sara: When they…when the union finally fought for us to have our own rooms, that was [the] greatest thing that could ever happen. If we had a man in our list, on our crew list, the man automatically got a free room...got a single room.

David: Got a single.

Sara: But the girls always had to share, so the union fought for us to get our own rooms.

David: I love that little hidden stuff in history people don't know about, that's fascinating. Chef, it's international time. So how did that happen? Tell me all about getting into the international.

Sara: Well, the international thing happened when Carl Icahn came along. He came along in ... 1986. He put us on furlough for about maybe two years, saying we weren't getting our jobs back, we weren't bread winners. We fought for two years without our jobs and then when we came back, he destroyed everything. Turned it into one system instead of having half international, half domestic which is kind of okay with us because now we got a chance to go international and that was alright with me. I just didn't want to commute. I never wanted to commute out of Chicago. Then I was forced to commute because ...he had closed Chicago. He closed a lot of our domiciles down, trying to save money or make money I should say.

Sara: Well, when I first got my international qualification, we had to go back to training and be qualified for overseas because I did have international training when I first went to training. They trained us both sides but I had...we had to go back and refresh it because we were now going on international. My international was I had to leave Chicago and commute to New York, which I did not want to do. I went on and did it anyway and I flew fifteen years straight international. Wasn't so bad; but I got used to it. It used to take me one solid day; I always had to give up one of my days to get to New York because now I have to get an apartment. I got an apartment with five other women. We had a two bedroom and we made our living room into a bedroom and put two beds in each room.

David: It was strictly get some rest and kick off.

Sara: That's right because we would do... He had a set up where as we could do an international flight in 24 hours we'd go back out on another one. Before that we always had a 24-hour layover.

David: You got a chance to...if you wanted to you could go check the town out where you were, you know?

Sara: Yes and we were able to do that and that was wonderful. I'd love my international flying because I flew London straight for fifteen years.

David: Tell me, out of all the countries you went, what were some of your favorite destinations and how were you treated when you were there as an African–American woman?

Sara: My favorite destination was Egypt because I was so junior and a lot of junior people didn't get a chance to fly international. We had women flying twenty-five and thirty years holding that line down; they wouldn't give it up for love or money. I don't blame them, because they had 24 hours sometimes 48-hour layovers there. They wasn't giving that up and they were working four times a month. That's a dream to work four times a month. Every now and then I would get a trip to Egypt and I tell you we stood out like sore thumbs.

David: Really? Why?

Sara: Yes, because number one we were Americans; number two we were Black Americans and we were young Black Americans. I [will] never forget my first time walking through the bazaar in Egypt

David: In Cairo?

Sara: In Cairo and I hear somebody say, "Sara!" I'm like...

David: Somebody called? I'm in Cairo who's that? What is this?

Sara: I turned around and looked and they... I said, "You were..." They say, "Oh we were a passenger on your airplane and you gave us our documentation."

David: Isn't that something.

Sara: I freaked out.

David: Isn't that something.

Sara: I freaked out. Then when we would walk... Because we still wore our uniform coats all the time so we always knew which places to go because once we hit the bazaar they knew us.

David: Right.

Sara: Because of our coats.

David: Absolutely.

Sara: They would come and get us, the Egyptians. I got a brother that sells this; let me take you to my cousin that sells this. That's how we got around in the bazaar.

David: You were treated very well there?

Sara: We were treated with kid gloves there.

David: Incredible.

Sara: One of the guys told me, he says, "Why don't you fly this more often? We're tired of seeing these old white women."

David: That's great.

Sara: I said, "I wish I could." By then I had fifteen years under the belt, so I wasn't a baby, you know?

David: Yes, you were an all-star. You knew the business.

Sara: Yes.

David: Tell me other places where maybe it wasn't quite that way.

Sara: London was... London life, they were pretty good to us; but I didn't like the way they treated the blacks that lived there. They treated us... I've seen them... I'll never forget this I was in a china store; I was buying some china and this one little black guy...

Sara: This is in London. This one little black guy, I think he was working the stock room. Well they talk to him so bad I just had... I said, "You know what? Why are they treating him so bad and they're treating us like royalty?" That's because we were spending our money and he was working for them. I didn't like that, but they always treated us even nice on the street. If we stood up on the street at a bus stop or at a... they called it the Tube.

David: The Tube.

Sara: We stood there trying to figure out our way they would immediately walk up to us and say, "Hey where are you going?" That's why I liked London because they spoke English and they would help you get to your destination.

David: Speaking of language, did you find in some of your travels that not being able to speak the home language was a huge barrier? Or was there... Did you figure out how to make it work anyway?

Sara: We figured how to make it work; especially Paris.

David: We all.

Sara: I loved Paris.

David: J'aime la Paris.

Sara: Don't even try to speak the language because they'll look at you and say you're destroying our beautiful language.

David: I've spent some time in Paris and they...

Sara: Yes they did not appreciate that.

David: They funny about that.

Sara: You point, you talk to them in English they'll figure it out but don't even try to mess with their language.

David: They get all sour looking, like...

Sara: Yes, but Italians was totally different.

David: How so?

Sara: The Italian people, they were excited to see us black women; but they didn't care if we tried to mangle their language or not. Italian men, they would follow us.

David: I'm sure.

Sara: They followed us. I was there one time with a girlfriend and we felt this guy following us for a quite a way. So finally we stopped and he caught up with us and he says, "Why are you walking so fast? Americans rush all the time. You're in Italy now. Sit back and relax and enjoy this country." Of course he wanted to take us to dinner and everything.

David: That's great.

Sara: That's a typical Italian man.

David: Let's take [it] through the countries, then. We have France... Italy. Did you go to different parts of Italy—Rome, Milan?

Sara: Well, we did go to Milan. We flew [to] Milan a lot. Milan was nice, too. The men there they just love black women.

David: They love the sisters, because they've got a little of us in them.

Sara: Right.

David: You know, Hannibal took care of that, you know, during the Roman conquest. What about Sweden or places like that?

Sara: Sweden, I spent some time there, but not a lot of time there. They were really nice. I didn't like Sweden too much, because it was so expensive, very expensive.

David: You were in Stockholm?

Sara: Stockholm. Very cold.

David: Yes, very cold. Now, how about places like Russia or...?

Sara: I got a chance to go to Berlin. That was another one of my favorite places.

David: Tell me. Why?

Sara: It was a young city, very young city.

David: Very vibrant.

Sara: Very vibrant.

David: Now, they were still East Berlin at that time.

Sara: You know, they had just tore the wall down. So I was able to go over and see part of the wall, pick up a piece, and bring it home.

David: Isn't that cool.

Sara: I enjoyed Berlin, especially around Christmas time. Because they went all the way out.

David: They do that, you know, Christmas celebration big time.

Sara: I enjoyed Berlin. I enjoyed Germany. Germany was... Now, I think Germany was a little more racist than any country. I don't know why...

David: Tell me. How so? It kind of felt different or...?

Sara: I felt like they didn't like us. I just felt it, you know. They never approached me or anything, but I could just tell. You feel uneasy...

David: Being black you...

Sara: You can feel it, your hair raises up, you know it's...

David: We can feel [it]. It's difficult to explain, but I've tried... You know, white folks don't know about this but we...

Sara: We can feel it.

David: Because we had to deal with this stuff for so long, we know. We can sense situations and it's very interesting.

Sara: Exactly. Another favorite city that I really enjoyed, [though] it scared the heck out of me... [was in] Israel.

David: Really?

Sara: Beautiful. We stayed by the water side, by the ocean. I'm telling you, my first night there I was freaking out because all I would hear was gunshots, airplanes circling over.

David: This was really when they were going at it hard with the Palestinians.

Sara: Exactly. What really threw me away was to see women in full dress, long skirts and machetes...guns with machetes on their backs, women. I said, "Oh, my Lord. What is going on here." There were certain places and areas that we could not go to.

Sara: They gave us briefings.

David: Here's where you can go, here's where you can't go. Here's a map. If you find yourself here, you better run.

Sara: They told us one thing: stay off public transportation because they were blowing up everything. I walked everywhere I went ... They put us in an area where there was a lot of shopping, you know. We could shop around and eat in different places. We were in a good area, but you still heard those guns, you still heard bombings. Even when we landed, they would tell us don't wear your uniform coats.

David: Because you're a target.

Sara: You're a walking target.

David: Did the Israeli people treat you differently?

Sara: They were nice to us. They were very nice to us. In fact, we stayed right down the street from the consulate, the American consulate. We stayed there. I felt comfortable there; but it was just weird.

David: It's a little scary when you're in a warzone like that.

Sara: Yes. It was real scary; but they were nice. They welcomed us, you know.

David: Fascinating. So any African or Caribbean places? Did you do anything like that?

Sara: I never made it to Africa, West Africa. I never made it to like, Nigeria, or anything like that.

David: Senegal or anything like that?

Sara: No.

David: Okay. What about Bahamas, you know, those kinds of places?

Sara: Briefly made it to the Dominican.

David: Tell me a little bit about the Dominican.

Sara: That really put something on my mind, because when we landed there [the] poverty was just unbelievable. You land in this airport with no walls. It's all open and the first thing you see is these little dirty black kids running up to you trying to take your bags and that's another thing they schooled us on. Do not let your bags out of sight, because if you do they're gone.

David: You're never going to see them.

Sara: That's right, so we had to always shoo them away. Don't give them any money, because you'll never get rid of them. Our hotel was close to the airport and they told us don't leave the airport's grounds because they rob people. I was kind of scared. I didn't stay that long in the Dominican; but we just stayed there at the airport.

David: Isn't that something. Well, we could get into why all that happened and how come certain countries are this way and so... But we want to spare the political stuff a little bit. I do want to ask you, in your experience, do you believe Black Americans are generally regarded with admiration, disdain or indifference in other countries?

Sara: Well I think they are…generally are admired.

David: Admired.

Sara: Because we come from such a rich country, you know. Our country is one of the richest countries, you know, and we have so much freedom. They do look up to us and sometimes we can go over there and act a pure ass.

David: The Ugly America.

Sara: I've heard that so many times and seen it.

David: But did black people?

Sara: No, white folks.

David: White folks just doing what they do.

Sara: That's right.

David: Thinking that they own some other place.

Sara: There you go. They would show out and then I'd hear them saying "Oh, the Ugly American." I hated that, you know, because they classed us all in one bunch.

David: Interesting.

Sara: Other places, like…Amsterdam was a wonderful place.

Sara: Wonderful place to go. I felt comfortable there and everybody helped, even though it was a language barrier there. But I just enjoyed myself there, never had any problems there. Right away they took you to the Light District. My first time… I'm like, "Why is she sitting up in there half naked and on display?"

Sara: That's the whole idea, you know. I enjoyed Amsterdam. It was just something beautiful to see, to actually see, a windmill; to actually see the wooden shoes and the tulips.

David: And the canals.

Sara: And the canals, just fascinating.

David: Interesting. All right well, we're going to get a little more political here. In your opinion is there a specific moment or period in the last four hundred years of our history that stands out as being the most important? If you think about the sweep of us in this country, is there any part of it that you think really in your thinking stands out the most?

Sara: They admired Dr. King over there. That's all you heard; but a lot of times they would bring him up. They admired him very much. So in Europe, I think all over Europe, [people] admired Dr. King.

David: All right, so you have a business here in the city. Why don't you talk a little bit about... how you got out of the flight thing and how you came into this.

Sara: Well American bought TWA back in 2001, I believe. I flew for American for about two years then they put us all on the bottom. I had almost thirty years by then. They put us all on the bottom and we're back to number one again where we would fly in puddle hoppers five lakes a day. I'm old now. I can't do that.

Sara: Once the airline was dissolved we could start collecting our pension. We collected our pension. They took us off and put us in the streets because we were the low man on the totem pole. They started cutting back. When they started cutting back, I had to do something; but I knew I wasn't going to go with another airline because I had already had thirty years in and I couldn't do anymore.

My sister, being a teacher at The Art Institute in Philadelphia, she taught fashion designing. She said, "Why don't you go on and go to school for culinary?" she said, "You can get a family discount." At this time ... the City of Saint Louis, being that TWA was based in Saint Louis, gave us a $10,000 reeducation fund.

I said, "You know what? I'm going to take advantage of that. It's only $10,000, but it's better than nothing. I did. I took advantage of that. I got my sister's family discount from The Art Institute and then I took that $10,000 (although they didn't pay it till I finally finished school). I went on to be retrained as a chef because I loved to cook. Even when I was flying I'd always bring food and everybody would gravitate to me.

David: Now we're going to shift a little bit more. All that travel, all of that, did that change you in anyway? Make you think differently about things?

Sara: It changed [me] a lot because we were a poor black family from Pittsburgh. Both my parents lived [there]...they both met in steel mills. In Pennsylvania, all the steel mills shut down. I relived it through my life. My parents at my age lost their jobs and now and I'm at their age losing my job. It was like history repeating itself. It made a big change in my life.

David: Tell me a little more about all that travel and everything. Did it open anything up for you?

Sara: It opened my eyes to see how the other side lived. We have so much to get. We've got so many resource, it's unbelievable. The people over in Europe, they don't have the resources that we have. We have the welfare, we have housing; a lot of those people don't have that what we have. It opened my eyes...

3. Marvinetta Penn –
Executive Director of Global Girls

I dream big and make those dreams come true. Once I knew that I could no longer totally devote myself to teaching, I quit. I traveled throughout Europe and sang in Dubai and Singapore before settling back in Chicago and starting Global Girls. I've taken eleven girls to Africa on three different trips. I've only just begun to win. I want to produce more of my own plays and have them published and performed all over the world, giving voice to girls and women who never knew that they had anything to say or that anyone cared to listen.

You Go Girl! Globally.

1. *What first brought you in contact with Black Americans (or people from other countries)? Have the relationships continued? If so, can you give any personal stories or experiences?*

As the executive director of Global Girls, I feel obligated to take young women of color to as many countries outside America as possible. As an African American woman who has traveled extensively and grown exponentially from international travel, I understand the impact trips to countries in Africa has had and will continue to have on my girls in Chicago and the girls we've visited in Ghana, Nairobi and Mombasa.

I've taken twenty-three girls on five separate trips to the continent. We've worked with hundreds of girls while in [the] country. The core of our work gives girls a voice to speak their personal truths, to own their feelings, to express their joys, fears, dreams and passions in a safe space.

While on our last trip to Mombasa, Kenya, we worked with one young lady whom none of us will forget. Zarie was a natural leader. With a ready smile and a glint of hope in her eyes, she recited the Global Girls Law with passion and commitment in every session. By the end of our week together, she was one of the few girls who knew the law by heart. She created steps for their final dance performance. She cajoled the other girls into working hard on their skit. Zarie even taught younger girls at her school, girls who were not a part of our program, our songs and games. When the eight of us from the Global Girls team visited the school, youth stood outside joyfully singing our songs as our bus approached. At the end of our time together, Zarie ran to the bus as it was pulling off and promised me that she would continue leading the girls in the Global Girls way and that she would remain "fearless".

I've worked with countless girls in the States. Not once had I encountered a Zarie. We are continuing our work with the girls in Mombasa through a partnership with Chicago-based Mombasa Relief Initiative.

2. *What would you say is the level-of-interest in Black Americans living outside the U.S. (Asia, Europe, Africa, etc.)? Do you feel Black Americans are socially accepted in these places?*

I believe that Black Americans who visit other countries and are authentically curious, who engage with others, who venture off the beaten path are welcomed by those who live in the country. Others, who go to see and be seen, are only socially accepted by others who want to see and be seen. I've traveled extensively and never felt shunned.

3. *How do your colleagues regard African Americans? Can you relate a specific story or experience that can illustrate your opinion?*

N/A

4. *In your country (or outside the U.S. in general) do you believe Black Americans are generally regarded with admiration, disdain or indifference? Why or why not? Have you ever heard the term "Ugly American" used to refer to a Black American? If yes, can you give an example?*

From my experience, its indifference. No one cares. The only thing that concerns most people either here or abroad is what another brings to the table that serves a need whether it is information, entertainment or of economic benefit.

People take who they are with them. For many African Americans, life has been about status, either inherited or gained. When those people travel, they take their status with them, I assume. For me, one who has no status, life is about being present in whatever moment I find myself. People who share that belief, that life view, will be attracted to me and will be in harmony. I guess it all boils down to the person and their focus or point of attraction.

5. *Outside the U.S. have opinions about Black Americans changed within the last decade? If so, why?*

I think so. Television and American movies are huge exports. Many people get their information about African Americans from those sources. However, they are still open to learning up close and personally from us. It is imperative that more of us travel so that people can see that we are not the buffoons or thugs and misfits portrayed in the mass media.

6. *While it is well-recognized the impact Black Americans have had on American culture (arts, literature, music, social justice movements, politics, etc.), what impact (if any) do you feel African Americans have had on culture outside the U.S.? How widely do you feel your view is shared in your home county (or where you live if living abroad)?*

N/A

7. *Are Black American leaders (both present and past) known your country, and if yes, how are they regarded? If you've lived abroad, how well are African Americans known those countries? Who would you say are the most highly-regarded Black American leaders outside the U.S.?*

N/A

8. *In your opinion, is there a specific moment or period in the past 400 years of African American history that stands out as being uniquely important?*

N/A

9. *Are there one or more African American individuals whose contributions have influenced your own thinking or activities?*

N/A

This last question requires a bit of background:

This is a pivotal point in modern history as the global political economy is shifting, American hegemony is being challenged, and many nations and cultures once-considered "underdeveloped" are coming to the forefront. While there is no question Black Americans have been vital to the political, economic, and social development of the United States from its inception through the 20th century, there is a widespread feel they have lost ground in the 21st century. Going forward Black Americans are at risk of remaining a marginalized minority as racial prejudices and poverty gain ground, and other ethnic groups fight for their share of America's shrinking base-of-resources.

Black Americans have consistently benefitted from relationships and dialogue with other cultures outside the U.S., just as have other cultures have been enrich by their experience with Black Americans.

10. *What insights, opinions, or perspectives would you give to African Americans in this uncertain era as they continue the struggle to repel racism, to maintain hard-won gains, and perhaps most importantly, find footage and advancement going forward?*

I am not the best person to give an opinion here as my life's work is deeply rooted in manifestation of love right here on earth. I've been exposed to racism, sexism, ageism, colorism, you name it "ism" and, "...still I rise." We have the power. If we take on the responsibility of desire turned into decision bolstered by deliberate action.

Teresa Córdova

Teresa Córdova is the Director of the Great Cities Institute (GCI) at the University of Illinois at Chicago. She teaches urban planning and policy in the College of Urban Planning and Public Affairs (CUPPA) and serves as affiliate faculty of UIC's Departments of Sociology, Gender and Women's Studies, and Latino and Latin American Studies. She received her PhD in sociology from the University of California, Berkeley.

As an elected or appointed member of a plethora of organizations—policy groups, grassroots organizations, regional and national boards, city and county governing bodies—Córdova has affected economic development policy and projects, the provision of infrastructure, local governance, and neighborhood change.

In 2015, Dr. Córdova was honored with the Sor Juana Legacy Award from the National Museum of Mexican Art. As an applied theorist, political economist, and community-based planner, Dr. Córdova approaches her work as a *scholarship of engagement, integrating research,* pedagogy and service.

Solidarity Revealed through Music

As a Chicana who was raised in the Southwest, it didn't take much for me to see the connections between experiences of black and brown folks—an understanding that has lasted a lifetime. I suppose my affinity with blacks in the United States started in my home with the sounds of my parents' LPs of Sara Vaughan and Nat King Cole and the television variety shows that featured these artists. Because of older siblings, some of my earliest memories of music were of early doo-wop. To this day, I still sing my first favorite songs, which I think are masterpieces of harmony and vocal creativity—"Earth Angel" (The Penguins 1955) and "Sincerely," (The Moonglows 1956)—at the top of my lungs, usually with my son, who, I'm fairly certain, loves them as much as I do.

Because I played the piano, Fats Domino was my favorite and through him, I developed an ear for music from New Orleans, learning to love Professor Longhair, Allen Toussaint, Dr. John and later Lee Dorsey. I was in heaven when, in the early 1960s, the girl groups hit the scene. I loved every song – and knew all the lyrics – of

The Marvelettes, The Shirelles, The Chiffons, The Ronettes, The Chantells, The Dixie Cups, Little Eva, Doris Troy, Mary Wells, and Barbara Lewis. Thanks to American Bandstand and Oklahoma City's KOMA, I had access to music I might not have otherwise heard. It was through this music that I felt deeply connected to blacks in this country whose spiritual expressions touched mine. But I wasn't the only one. Other Chicanos were making the same connections as black and brown solidarity was emerging. Later in the decade of the 1960s, bands like Tower of Power from Oakland and War from L.A. represented that alliance and the music of Santana highlighted Afro-Latino influences.

The songs that most stirred my soul were Sam Cooke's "A Change is Gonna Come" (1964) and Curtis Mayfield and the Impressions' "People Get Ready" (1965). On Friday, July 24, 1964, triggered by reports of brutality leveled against an intoxicated nineteen year old, a "riot" broke out in the streets of Rochester, New York. For the next several years, in cities across the United States, reports of police harassment and brutality led to what is widely referred to as "urban race riots." Though the media accounts of these uprisings have been analyzed and criticized, it was through the daily television accounts in the mid 1960s, that I watched beatings and head bashings of Black Americans. I had already read about the atrocities of slavery, but as a teenager, I was witnessing via television the inhumanity to which black people in this country were still subjected. I heard many expressions of sympathy from my parents. They knew far too well the oppressions faced by Mexican Americans. After the 1967 "riots" in Detroit, President Lyndon Johnson appointed the National Advisory Commission on Civil Disorders (The Kerner Commission). It was not surprising that fifty years after the release of the Commission's report (February 29, 1968) I would organize an event to commemorate this historic moment and highlight the perpetuation of conditions described in the report.

As a teenager, it wasn't hard for me to find a job. One of the advantages of slow – usually snowy - nights when I was a "carhop" at the A&W Root Beer was that I could stuff the jukebox. Because the small restaurant was located at the bottom of the hill from the local junior college, I also had many interactions with their winning basketball team that just a couple of years earlier, included Spencer Hayward. Besides the family that owned a local tire shop and the athletes attending the junior college, there had not been many blacks in this area since the early days of coal mining.

My first job away from home was in housekeeping at the Cosmopolitan Hotel in Denver, Colorado, where I worked alongside African American women, most of whom lived in the Five Points neighborhood of Denver, where many Chicanos also lived. I remember how nice these women were to me. I appreciated their guidance in the work of cleaning hotel rooms. I was very proud when—only after a few weeks—I was assigned my own floors to clean. It was only a couple of years later that I was accepted by University of Denver professors Charles Cortese and Frank Falk to be part of a National Science Foundation funded research project to examine residential segregation theories by comparing the Park Hill neighborhood with Five Points. Of course, I had no fear of being in the neighborhoods and always returned with the highest numbers of completed survey questionnaires. (Years later, I would playfully challenge my students to keep up with me in conducting door-to-door surveys.) My enthusiasm for the research process was certainly a motivator, but my ability to connect to the people in Five Points reinforced for me the importance of not doing research "on" people but with them, or at the very least, with their support.

When I arrived in Berkeley to attend graduate school in sociology, the gravitational pull was not just to other Chicanos, but to Puerto Ricans and other students of color. The alliance was natural and the connections around cultural expressions such as humor were immediate. So were our values, priorities and reasons for being in graduate school. Professor Troy Duster (grandson of Ida B. Wells), through the Institute for the Study of Social Change, provided mentorship and a home for dozens of students studying various aspects of race and social change. David Montejano taught one of my first courses at Berkeley on theories of social change, during which I learned about the restructuring of an economic system (from feudalism to capitalism). My own interests in social change were solidified.

Through our activism in student and city government, students of color and "progressive whites" at Berkeley coalesced in 1984 to organize the twentieth anniversary of the Free Speech Movement (FSM) and recognizing our abilities to organize large rallies, embarked on anti-apartheid activities in solidarity with blacks in South Africa fighting against the system of apartheid. Parallel to our fight for divestment by the University of California from companies in South Africa, we also coalesced around affirmative action policies, the formation of a graduate student union and solidarity work with Central America and Grenada. I taught a course called, "Empowering Women of Color: Issues and Actions in Affirmative Action," out of which myself and my students organized the first *Empowering Women of Color Conference* (1985), which is still held every year on the Berkeley campus. Organizing this conference was on the heels of my work with other Latinas in universities in Northern California to form Mujeres Activas en Letras y Cambios Social (MALCS)

(Women Active in Letters and Social Change).

Besides our work on campus, several of us were involved with city government, where Eugene "Gus" Newport was the first black mayor (and the only one since). Nancy Skinner, who had been the chair of the Graduate Assembly (graduate student government), was a city councilor. Later Pedro Noguera, also chair of the Graduate Assembly, and president of the Associated Students of the University of California, Berkeley was an elected member of the Berkeley School Board. I was on the Berkeley Planning Commission and before I left for my first stint in Chicago, was playing a key role in working with Mayor Newport and his staff on revitalization without displacement strategies for South Berkeley, the African American neighborhood in Berkeley.

Despite how active I was in Berkeley, it was the draw of the black/Latino/ progressive white coalition in Chicago, which led to the election of Harold Washington, that motivated me to accept the opportunity to move to Chicago and teach in the Latin American Studies program at the University of Illinois at Chicago (UIC), where I was the first Latina to teach in the program. My first public presentation at UIC in 1986 was at a symposium on Black/Latino coalitions. I later wrote a paper, which appeared in a volume edited by David Montejano, *Chicano Politics and Society in Late Twentieth Century* (1999), on "Harold Washington and the Rise of Latino Electoral Politics in Chicago, 1982–1987."

I left Chicago after a few years. It would be twenty-one years before I would return to the city to direct the Great Cities Institute at the University of Illinois. In the interim, among my many activities as an activist scholar, I worked closely with the Environmental Justice Movement, which at its core was a coalition of people of color affected by the disproportionate impacts from the siting of toxic facilities, who were fighting for healthy communities. More recently, I served on the board of the Praxis Project for nine years, seven of which as president. Throughout the United States, the Praxis Project works with community organizers in communities of color and provides technical assistance, research, and financial support towards the wellbeing of communities.

I've been around enough young men of color to know that not having access to good jobs and opportunities is a major force in affecting their sense of dignity and in turn their behavior choices. Finding decent jobs didn't seem to be as easy for them as it had been for me. Prior to returning to Chicago, through the Resource Center for Raza Planning, I worked with a community development corporation to develop a small business incubator and was in the midst of developing a youth entrepreneurship program. So when I returned to Chicago, I was already scoped to observe joblessness among young people in Chicago, particularly African American men. I had made it known that Great Cities Institute (GCI) was interested in producing reports for the hearings on youth employment held at the Chicago Urban League and sponsored by Alternative Schools Network and other community organizations. so I jumped at the opportunity when asked to produce reports on employment to population ratios and out of school, out of work figures.

Alexia Elejalde-Ruiz, a journalist with the *Chicago Tribune*, did such an amazing job of conveying the essence and depth of our reports' findings and conclusions through front page articles, that the significance of our research resonated and shocked many in the region. They were compelled to turn their attention to addressing the "chronic and concentrated" conditions of joblessness, particularly for those who lived in the neighborhoods "abandoned" by the flight of "industry and opportunity." Our reports showed, for example, that in the city of Chicago, nearly half of African American men between the ages of 20-24 were neither in school, nor employed. Focusing on joblessness was a way to address the conditions that remain after the devastating impacts of the decline of the manufacturing industry from places that had grown around the demand for labor. Once that labor force was no longer required at the same rates, little effort was made to incorporate the discarded labor in a restructuring economy. Massive incarceration of surplus labor replaced an employed labor force.

Stretching back to my first formal research experience examining residential segregation in the Five Points and Park Hill neighborhoods, these reports exemplified my life-long commitment to *harnessing the power of research* (a GCI tagline) to positively affect conditions for good living. This research was much more than an academic exercise for met as a brown woman. It was an outgrowth of a deep empathy for the black and brown young men and women in our communities.

Addressing conditions of joblessness in communities devastated by the loss of economic activity and the erosion of social fabrics was also a way to address the ramifications of something I have been studying over the last forty years as it has been unfolding, namely, economic restructuring of the economy. I wrote about in an article published in *Aztlán: A Journal of Chicano Studies*, entitled "The Regime of Neoliberal Policies and the Implications for Latino Studies Scholarship." In this article and in talks I give on the subject, after describing the logic of how the economic system functions, I describe three major characteristics of the restructuring process: increasing profit from the production process (e.g. the search for cheaper labor costs); a push for the withdrawal of the state from establishing regulatory frameworks and providing social benefits (the decline of the welfare capitalism); and accelerated international activities, especially those related to the expansion of global capital (globalization).

I insist that we must view these political economic dynamics as a context to understand the conditions in our communities including industrial, occupational, neighborhood and government restructuring that has created both job loss and lower wages; displacement caused by disinvestment and gentrification; debt bondage; decreased access to affordable housing, education and social services; increased social control (e.g. incarceration) and militarization of policing; increased social ills including substance abuse, domestic violence and violence in the streets; and disruption of local economies and cultures in countries in the Global South. When we understand these dynamics, then we will also understand that black and brown labor and environmental resources have been exploited and extracted as key ingredients for the functioning of the neoliberal economy today as well as colonial economies of previous eras. Colonialism in Africa, the Americas and Asia has often been called a "crime against humanity," even more recently, by the perpetrators of the colonial violence (e.g. the president of France in 2017) and set the stage for institutionalized discrimination evident today.

By understanding this context, we can understand why black and brown people, including indigenous communities, are natural allies. Succumbing to the forces that attempt to divide us is counterproductive for each of our communities. For example, it makes no sense for blacks in the United States to succumb to the ideologically manipulated message that the reason that African Americans face conditions of joblessness is because of Mexican immigrants. And while more and more Latino groups are embracing their indigenous roots, they are also acknowledging that Afro Latinos in their communities is a reminder that more enslaved Africans were transported to the Caribbean, Mexico, and Central and South America than to areas that became the United States of America and that they supplemented the exploited labor of indigenous people of the Americas. Not commonly known, is that Mexican Americans and Native Americans in the Southwestern United States share a common history with African Americans of being terrorized and lynched.

"Back in the day," of the late 1960s and 1970s, The Chicano, Puerto Rican Independence, Native American, and Black Power movements often worked together in solidarity and mutual support because they understood the history and realities of why we needed to be connected. It was more than just a litany of disadvantage, but a deep understanding of the source of oppression. Angela Davis, in a recently released film by Peter Bratt on Dolores Huerta, *Dolores,* said,

Often times today, looking back, we think about discreet and distinct movements. We think that the Black Movement was one movement and the Chicano Movement was over here. And then there was the Native American Movement. But all of those movements and the individuals within those movements were connected and we knew that one movement would not be successful without the other. Today we talk about the intersectionality of struggles, but I think during that period, we actually lived it; we experienced it.

Luis Valdez, a filmmaker and founder of El Teatro Campesino (Farmworkers' Theatre), expressed something similar in the same film:

It became really apparent that the racism that touches black people was no different than the racism that touches the other groups. So we were really marching for everybody, we were really marching for social change.

The grape boycott, led by Cesar Chavéz and Dolores Huerta, in the interest of farmworkers in California attempting to unionize, was one of the most successful examples of a broad based coalition coming together to stand against powerful interests, such as the growers of California's agricultural fields.

It is from a perspective of connection and solidarity that I view my relationship to African Americans in the United States. To me, our struggles are the same, even with their different iterations. These shared struggles are also the basis for a shared commitment to change the conditions that oppress not only our people, but any and all people who suffer the plight of an economic system that enriches some while impoverishing others. I believe that we need to continue to see ourselves as connected, as allies against a common enemy. Blacks in the United States can benefit from the acknowledgement of our historical connections and not allow the finite pie argument to pit us against one another. United, with understanding, we have a better chance to prevail.

Today, I still listen to oldies, but I also listen to the hip hop out of New York City, whose roots are both Puerto Rican and African American; the Jamaican inspired reggae music from Argentina; the Afro-Latino beats of the Caribbean; the Chicano Movement bands of Malo and El Chicano; the blues inspired music of Indigenous and Los Lonely Boys; rhythmic Soukous from Africa; the heartfelt ballads of Mexico, and of course, Chicago Blues. Our cultural connections, as heard through music, reveal a deep and continued history of solidarity that when we build upon it, can lead to positive social change. Si Se Puede!

l-r   John Woodford, Exective Editor, U of Michigan publications; Dr. Frank Morris, Morgan State U; Vladimir Nadeen, Russian journalist; Rafael Moseev, Russian journalist, Professor Jan Carew, Northwestern University

CATECHISM OF HOPE   for Sheila, Anne, Sekou, Beverly.

by Jan Carew

*For Alice with
fraternal good wis-
Jan.*

If you stumble and fall down

before our struggle's won

don't pine any longer

than it takes

for tears to tie themselves

like shoelaces under your chin;

and don't believe for a moment

that flowers won't bloom again

or kiskadees won't sing,

that rivers of the morning

won't sparkle

under the lash of winds,

that mists won't be trapped

like the breath of dreamtime seekers

in fastnesses of dark green hills,

that the Road to Hope

will glitter for an instant

and then crumble

like the skin

a snake leaves behind him,

that mimosas will deny their perfume

to long cool evenings.

If you stumble and fall down

before our struggle's won,

stand up,

wash and bandage your wounds,

FROM HERE

rustin

spit blood and sing

through a swollen mouth,

sing a wild song

and let it echo

in vortices of your head

like a bellbird's fife, panpipe or flageolot

or like a talking drum.

Stand up, I said

and let the wild sun bandage your eyes,

and when you burst asunder the bandage

with bare hands,

cross ten thousand seasons of pain

between dayclean and can't-see-time,

feeling good,

singing a refrain

of the born again fighter,

and when night staggers in

like a drunken priest

burying the sun

rinse out your brain again and again

under a shower of stars.

Don't be afraid of catching cold,

the watchman of dayclean

will turn off the spigot in time

and you'll be ready, primed

to face ten million mornings

of a New Day.

Evanston October 8th. 1978

Printed with permission
from Dr. Joy Glesson Carew

Briefing for African-American, Latino and Native American leaders at UN Headquarters, New York city during Secretary General Kofi Annan's tenure in the 1990's.

Front row l-r (2nd from left) - Retired Air Force pilot James Graves; 4th from left Chicago journalist Nate Clay; 5th fron left Dr. Carol Adams
2nd row l-r (1st on left) - New Mexico State Senator Leonand Tsosi (Navajo Nation)
2nd row (2nd from left) - Angela Benally, Director of Indian Cultural Center Albuquerque, New Mexico
Front row far right - Illinois State Representative Lou Jones

Organized by the People Programme